TEACH YOUR
SON OR DAUGHTER
TO DRIVE

TEACH YOUR
SON OR DAUGHTER
TO DRIVE

by

David Hough

PAPERFRONTS
ELLIOT RIGHT WAY BOOKS
KINGSWOOD, SURREY, U.K.

Typeset in 10pt Times Roman by
EMS Photosetters, Rochford, Essex.
Made and Printed in Great Britain by Cox and Wyman, Reading.

CONTENTS

TO FIONA
Who passed first time

INTRODUCTION

HOW TO USE THIS BOOK

This book is designed to assist both the LEARNER DRIVER and the NON-PROFESSIONAL DRIVING INSTRUCTOR. Some sections aid the learner. Others lay out lesson plans and aid the instructor. At relevant stages the instructor is asked to give the book to the learner to work through the following sections until asked to give the book back. Those sections consist of essential principles of driving which the learner must know. The points at which the book is to change hands are clearly indicated throughout.

The book is planned as a complete integrated teaching package. Do not be tempted to rush through or miss out any part. There is no harm in the learner reading through the instructor's sections before his Driving Test but this should be discouraged too early on.

"Learn to drive with ease" says one driving school advertisement. "Pass your Test the simple way" says another. Both of these are dangerous assertions. For most people, learning to drive is not easy. Trying to fool potential customers does no one any good. On the basis that it's easy, the learner who passes may wrongly assume he is now expert and take risks; the learner who fails may wrongly conclude he is a personal failure.

Learning to drive demands good co-ordination and sound judgment, but nothing most adults cannot learn provided they are taught well.

Possibly the best way to learn to drive is with a comprehensive series of lessons by the finest reputed professional driving instructor you can find. But that will cost a tidy sum of money which not everyone can afford.

That is why around half of the thousands of people who take the Driving Test have always been, and will continue to be, taught to drive by amateurs. Almost all who pay for professional tuition in any case supplement their formal lessons with practice under the guidance of amateurs – friends or relatives. Let me hasten to explain that 'amateur' refers to that person's status as an instructor, not as a driver. Many amateur instructors are among the safest, most experienced drivers, able to teach way beyond the requirements of the Test.

This book is designed to take that 'amateur' or non-professional instructor and his learner through a co-ordinated series of lessons. It breaks down learning to drive into small digestible chunks, each explained in simple terms, followed up with stage-by-stage practice. It aims to draw together GOOD TEACHING, GOOD LEARNING, and GOOD LESSONS. It therefore shows the instructor how to get the best out of his learner and make the whole task enjoyable, at the same time showing the learner how to get the best value from his lessons.

The book can also be used to complement professional instruction. You need not fear mixing the teaching of the amateur with that of the professional (a good professional) because the latter should be used to dealing with learners of differing standards and stages of learning. One word of **warning**: a non-professional must not charge. Only a qualified professional driving instructor may accept payment for driving instruction.

Throughout the book I use 'he' when referring to both learner and instructor. This is purely for ease of writing and is in no way intended to cause offence. For the purposes of the title, readers will deduce that I envisaged the learner as a youngster, male or female, being taught by a parent or relative. However, I have aimed the book equally at those wanting to teach an older adult, perhaps a wife, husband, or friend.

PART ONE

PREPARATION

1

THE INSTRUCTOR

Many instructors come to grief through lack of preparation. So before you begin please read this. Your job is to help your learner to learn to drive. The important word is 'help'. You cannot learn for him. He needs both to gain KNOWLEDGE and develop UNDERSTANDING of it, and then put that into PRACTICE. Notice the order. If your learner starts driving before he understands what to do, you can count on problems! This book shows you what to teach and how, together with guidance on the degree of practice needed on each aspect.

But you need to do more than just teach. You must provide ENCOURAGEMENT and SUPPORT. How can you do that?

1. Try to see things from your learner's point of view. He may experience problems with things which seem patently obvious to you, things you've forgotten how you learned. The common mistake is to assume something ought to be as easy for him as for you.

2. Be patient. Mistakes will happen. To react with anger or alarm will only make matters worse. How to handle mistakes is covered shortly.

3. Give praise as well as criticism. It is easy to criticise and so easy to forget to praise. At the end of every lesson always try to find something to praise, or at least some words of encouragement. Try to end the lesson on a high note of optimism. Never let your learner go away in a cloud of gloom.

4. Stay calm. Resist the temptations to swear at the road hog who cuts in, to wave a fist at the idiot who sits on your tail. Such behaviour will have a bad effect upon your learner. It's not easy to stay relaxed, but teaching a learner driver never was easy. Be suspicious of anyone who tells you differently.

5. Watch your learner's reactions. Supportive teaching means watching for small signs on each drive and being prepared to handle them tactfully. For example is he: uneasy, nervous, worried, lacking in confidence, showing signs of tiredness, or simply afraid?

What sorts of clues give away such feelings? Look out for: reluctance to begin a lesson, worried facial expressions, dejected posture, panic symptoms, evasive responses to your questions, unsteady hands, talking out of character.

If your learner appears ill-at-ease before you get into the car, stop and delay the lesson. Listen to what's wrong over a cup of tea. That way you should identify the problem. Then you should be able to restore confidence by first going back to the stage of learning which is needing extra help.

In this respect the friend/relative beats the commercial driving instructor. The latter is paid and is thus obliged to get on and give the lesson. He has less time to pause and put his learner at ease.

If extreme concern appears while you are out on the road, ask your learner to pull over to the side as soon as safely possible. After the engine switch-off routine give him a little "space", perhaps with a walk up and down outside the car together, if he needs it, to try to tell you what is causing the problem. *He* has to come to terms with his fears, not you. It may not be just one simple worry he needs to unload.

6. Each lesson in this book begins with a statement of its objectives. They define what the learner should be able to do by the end of that lesson. Make sure you know exactly what the objectives are and stick to them. Don't be tempted to extend them. Trying to achieve too much too soon is a common error.

Tell your learner the objectives in the lesson briefing. At the end of the lesson refer back to the objectives. If your learner has not achieved some, repeat them before going on to the next lesson. You may have to repeat certain things again and again until both of you are confident about them and happy to press on to the next stage. Beware of impatience in yourself or your learner which could land you in situations for which your learner is unready. Precious confidence would be shattered.

7. How frequent lessons should be, will depend mainly upon your learner. Some react well to intensive instruction and could run through the complete course in one week. But they are exceptional. Most will need time to consolidate and reflect on each stage of their learning. You must decide between you what frequency of lessons will be best. In round terms an average learner who needed around thirty hours of practice might complete the programme during a period of two months. The right amount of practice ultimately depends upon the individual. Most learners need at least the same number of driving hours as their age. Double that number would not go amiss. The point is that your learner must get sufficient 'driving miles' under his belt to become competent.

8. I return to mistakes.

DANGEROUS MISTAKES

These must be PREVENTED. For example:-
  (a) Your learner has failed to notice a child on the pedestrian crossing ahead; he is not slowing down.
  (b) Your learner is starting to move away without having noticed a cyclist about to pass the car.
  (c) Your learner, in the face of oncoming traffic, is about to pass a parked car with insufficient room alongside it to do so.

Act quickly to PREVENT dangerous mistakes. DON'T panic. DON'T lose your temper. DON'T grab the steering wheel. Simply tell your learner calmly, but firmly:-
  (a) to slow down and stop at the crossing.
  (b) not to move away yet.
  (c) to slow up and wait well back from the car until the

approaching traffic clears.

Once the mistake is corrected you need to find out why it occurred otherwise it could happen again. How long will you wait before you discuss it? That depends upon the nature of the fault and the situation at the time. Clearly you do not stop in the middle of a busy High Street holding up the traffic while the other motorists look on! Nevertheless make it as soon as possible. You must establish what was going on in your learner's mind when the mistake happened. Ask questions in a friendly manner to identify HIS line of thinking at that time. Resist simply TELLING him straightaway what he did wrong and what he should have done. Far better to ASK him what he *now* thinks he ought to have done so that he can establish for himself what went wrong and you can determine why the error was made and how to tackle it. It may be that he failed to pick up an important point in an earlier lesson or that he has been previously misinformed. Perhaps he simply forgot. Whatever it is, you must know why the problem arose before you can correct it effectively.

BAD HABITS

Your learner, during his life as a passenger, will have picked up certain conceptions of how a driver should behave. If a teenager's parents ignore seat belts he is likely to do the same. If a husband constantly ignores the speed limit his wife may be tempted likewise. These are bad habits, dangerous or not.

Bad habits must be CORRECTED STRAIGHTAWAY. Allow a bad habit to continue and your learner may assume that it is acceptable. For example a hand permanently resting on the gear lever prevents instant steering response. It has to be stopped.

If a bad habit is also dangerous it must be PREVENTED. Suppose you know that your learner is a chain smoker. You must refuse to teach him unless the cigarettes are left at home.

MISTAKES WHICH SHOULD BE SELF-CORRECTING

There is no need to prevent or correct all classes of mistake immediately, unless there is some element of danger or bad habit. Firstly, there is the type of error where the consequences show up later. Suppose your learner has pushed the choke most of the way home but he has forgotten that last little bit which advances the throttle. You have pointed this out to him before so this time you decide to let him find out himself. You let it ride because the next time he stops, the sound of the engine will bring home the point. Secondly, there is the fault purely due to lack of practice. Suppose your learner has yet to master synchronising clutch and accelerator when changing gear. In consequence he over-revs the engine from time to time. The fault should disappear with practice. Intervention now will achieve nothing.

LESSON BRIEFING

A couple of years ago I was in hospital undergoing a test known as an angiogram. It involved pumping a dye into my heart and then X-raying the progress of that dye around my artery system. Unfortunately the dye caused my heart to slow down and I felt myself slipping away . . . The solution was simple; all I had to do to clear the clogging dye from my heart was cough. But no one had ensured I knew how to handle what might happen! Once he realised the omission the surgeon gave a frantic shout, "Cough!" and I obliged. Imagine how much less disturbing it would have been had I been properly briefed.

I am not suggesting your learner will lose his grip on life without your lesson briefing but . . . do tell him the objectives for the particular lesson, where it will take place (at home, in traffic, etc.), what standard you expect, and remind him of points from previous lessons needing to be reinforced. Use the briefing to put your learner at ease too.

SEQUENCE OF TEACHING

No one can learn to drive in one go. Inevitably learners begin with less than total competence, which is why they have to display 'L' plates. You must minimise risk to other road users and yourselves by ensuring your learner builds up ability in the right sequence. Your aim is for prior understanding of every skill before it is met and needed on the road.

The sequence in this book is planned with full regard for educational theory and practice. Each section fits into a logical ordered whole with no new fact ever being dependent on one that hasn't been seen already. Most of the sequence is therefore naturally 'set in concrete'. However, learners' abilities and road conditions differ somewhat more than a book can always allow, and you may prefer to introduce a particular concept ahead of the plan. For example, I leave night driving until Lesson 10 but you may decide you have to introduce it earlier. If so, jump ahead and read the lesson concerned out of sequence.

EMERGENCY STOP

There is no clear-cut answer to when to teach the Emergency Stop because of two conflicting facts. On the one hand a learner can meet an emergency on his first day. On the other a day-old learner has little or no judgment of what is a driving emergency. There is a real risk of him jamming on the brakes and causing an accident when normal braking would suffice.

Different instructors teach the Emergency Stop at different stages. Commercial instructors tend to leave it to near the end of a course of instruction. They have the advantage of dual controls. It also saves them wear and tear on the school car.

In this programme of lessons your learner will begin Quick-Reaction Stops during the first lesson in which he makes the car move. He will build up to a full Emergency Stop before he goes amongst busy traffic. In all his learning you are having to balance your learner's inexperience against the safety of others. Keep reminding yourself, from the comfort of your instructor's seat, that your learner is almost bound to misjudge an emergency somewhere. It's no use if you are not awake to prompt in time.

NOW HAND THIS BOOK TO YOUR PUPIL

2

THE LEARNER

A great deal of personal discipline is required if you really want to pass your Test first go. No professional sportsman ever succeeded without it. On a more mundane level, my son would never have learned to play the cornet without the discipline of hours of practice. You should enjoy learning but you are not going to become an expert overnight. If this disappoints you, please stop and think about your attitude towards driving. Maybe you have been misled into expecting too much too soon . . .

You must anticipate making your share of mistakes. Your instructor will know how to deal with them. Try not to let yourself be put off by having made them. If your instructor seems to demand tough standards remember he wants you to pass too! And you can do it!

However, your instructor cannot pass the Test for you. He can help you learn only to the extent you are willing; the learning itself has to be by you. Please don't act like one young man who failed his Driving Test and immediately blamed the examiner. The examiner was right to fail him. His approach from the start had been to reject all advice on how to drive safely on the grounds he knew better, and it showed. Unless he changes his tune he will fail again, which is a pity. He is just not learning. I only mention him because too many youngsters spoil their chances in just the same way.

EFFECTIVE LEARNING

The lessons in this book are in a planned sequence. At the beginning of each one its objectives are listed. You will therefore be able to judge progress by reference to those objectives. This should make it easy to repeat things you agree you find difficult, and to avoid going on to the next lesson until you are ready. Should you at any stage feel impatient to learn more quickly and confident you could do so, rather than jump out of sequence and risk missing vital steps in your build-up of knowledge, see if you and your instructor can increase the frequency of your lessons.

However, as with most skills, it is best to learn a little at a time. For that very reason, instead of leaving the Highway Code to "cram" in at the end, this book shows on which parts to concentrate as you go along.

Listen to your instructor. Dad, uncle or neighbour, he's giving up his time for free! Let me extend here what I mean by "listen". It means arriving fresh. Time each lesson to avoid, for instance, when you are tired at the end of a busy day. You will progress faster in a relaxed frame of mind. Always visit the lavatory to make yourself comfortable before you drive. Fidgeting on that score can upset concentration considerably. It means avoiding alcohol. Any hangover symptoms will ruin a lesson – besides, at least one learner driver has been breathalysed and prosecuted!

Not to smoke during a lesson hardly needs saying in terms of "listen", with the irritation smoke can cause. In any case smoking stops you keeping both hands on the steering wheel. And imagine the danger were you to drop a lighted cigarette in your lap.

Between lessons you can improve your learning in several ways. Draw a diagram of the area surrounding your local High Street. Add some traffic. As the driver of each vehicle, what would *you* be looking for? What signals would you give? What traffic priorities must you respect? Some questions to note for your instructor are almost sure to arise. Whenever you are a passenger discuss traffic situations met, with the driver. You mustn't distract but you can still watch every detail just as carefully as the driver and try to understand why he does what he does.

The next thing is to plan strategy, when to start, etc.

FIRST GIVE THIS BOOK BACK TO YOUR INSTRUCTOR

3

JOINT PREPARATION

Half an hour at home in a relaxed atmosphere over a cuppa is worth sparing to set the tone. It provides the opportunity to compare attitudes and opinions on driving, to agree a lesson timetable, and to harmonise expectations of progress.

TOPICS TO DISCUSS
1. Why does your learner want to become a driver?
2. How quickly do *each* of you hope he can learn?
3. What does he look for from you as instructor?
4. What do you expect from him?
5. What problems does he anticipate?
6. What problems do you anticipate?
7. What will happen if he finds himself unable to cope?
8. What key learning factors can you recount from your own 'L' plate days?
9. In what order will the course of lessons be, and could that sequence shorten if progress is fast?
10. When should your learner apply for a Test?

Be prepared for the sorts of questions your learner may ask; for example, in relation to Topic 7 you will be able to explain that the systematic lessons make such a situation unlikely but that, should it happen, you will calmly issue precise instructions on how to recover in the particular circumstances. As a last resort, you might have to knock the car out of gear and pull on the handbrake, but that would only be if there was insufficient time otherwise to avert immediate danger. (See page 42.)

For some of the other topics you will need to glance through the rest of the book before your discussion takes place.

PROGRESS CHART

If you draw up a Progress Chart on the lines of fig. 1 you can keep efficient track throughout the lessons, of progress and of what needs more practice or revision. It will be a few moments well spent. You can use the chart alongside your diary but if you happen to fill in a future lesson-date at the

PROGRESS CHART

LESSON No.	DATE	NOTES (Important items which need revising. Objectives which are causing difficulty.)

Fig. 1

start of one lesson, leave out the number of the next lesson in case you need to repeat part or all of the earlier lesson first.

Before going on to the lessons, your learner must obtain an up-to-date Highway Code.

PART TWO

LESSONS

An approximate time is given for each lesson. Longer lessons should be divided by short breaks. However, it is important that your learner takes each lesson at his own pace. If he needs longer, fine. Make sure he never spends too long studying or more than a one-hour spell at the wheel. If he needs less time – also fine – provided he really has achieved the lesson objectives. Aim to achieve that important balance between pushing your trainee too hard, and allowing him to get bored.

LESSON 1

BEFORE TAKING THE WHEEL

OBJECTIVES
For your learner to be able to:-

1. Describe the basic Highway Code rules about drivers and their vehicles.
2. Relate six essential legal requirements of motorists.
3. Identify key controls and instruments from the driving seat, and state how they work.
4. Understand the clutch and transmission system.
5. Get safely into the driving seat of a car parked at the roadside.

DURATION and LOCATION

Approximately an hour and a half at home, including breaks, and a little time sitting in the car together to go over the controls.

BRIEFING

Before your learner begins, mention that you will give him a short quiz at the end. Explain that although the lesson is mainly self-study for him with which you won't interfere, you will remain on hand to answer queries, as well as for when he is ready to examine the driving controls in the car itself. Make sure that he has his up-to-date Highway Code, plus the instruction handbook for the car if possible. Something to write with is helpful too. Lastly, run over the objectives. This lesson is intended to make sure he is equipped with fundamental knowledge of driving, without which he cannot begin.

Note:

Find out about the controls from the maker's instruction handbook before you go over them together in the car. This makes remembering what's what much easier for your pupil, especially if he is not very mechanically minded. Much relevant extra information will be gathered at the same time. However, if you can't find it or borrow one, or you both prefer to make do without, see page 28.

PASS BOOK BACK TO PUPIL

This lesson introduces Rules of the Road and how a car works.

WHAT IS THE HIGHWAY CODE?

The Highway Code is not the law. Indeed one Road Traffic Act states that: "A failure on the part of a person to observe a provision of the Highway Code shall not of itself render that person liable to criminal proceedings of any kind". But this doesn't let you out of obeying the rules in the Highway Code! You can still be prosecuted, for example, for reckless driving with the charge backed by evidence that you ignored a single Highway Code rule. So be warned!

The first few Highway Code rules you must learn concern matters a driver must always consider before he begins a journey, any journey, not just his first driving lesson! They come at the start of the Highway Code section addressed to the Road User On Wheels. Please look there under the three sub-headings labelled: General; Alcohol and the road user; Seat belts.

You can condense these to make them easier to remember. Look at the following and cross-refer each rule to its full version in the Code:

* ★ Keep your vehicle in good condition.
* ★ Ensure loads are securely fastened.
* ★ Do not drive if you are unwell.
* ★ Do not drive if you are under the influence of drugs.
* ★ Use spectacles to correct defective vision.
* ★ Do not use tinted lenses in poor visibility.
* ★ Do not apply tinting materials to car windows.
* ★ Do not drink and drive.
* ★ Use a seat belt.
* ★ Restrain children with seat restraints.
* ★ Do not carry children in the luggage space.

or you can even abbreviate further:-

DO KEEP YOUR	— IN GOOD CONDITION
CAR	— PROPERLY LOADED
DO USE	— SPECTACLES IF REQUIRED
	— A SEAT BELT
	— RESTRAINTS ON CHILDREN
DO NOT DRIVE	— IF UNWELL
	— IF AFFECTED BY DRUGS
	— AFTER DRINKING
DO NOT	— REDUCE VISION WITH TINTED LENSES/GLASS
	— CARRY CHILDREN IN LUGGAGE SPACE

Despite these rules being cut down to size, the Highway Code message remains. If it helps you learn the standards the Code demands of you, you can adopt a similar process. Because it is always the message, rather than specific words, that you must know.

In my shortened list, I gave you five DOs and five DON'Ts. Cover them up while you jot them down. Check your answers against the original rules in the Code. If you have ten, or even all eleven, correct, you really are on the ball!

WHAT LEGAL REQUIREMENTS AFFECT DRIVERS?

1. You must be at least 17 years old.

2. You must have a current provisional driving licence. You can apply for it up to two months early. Application forms are at local post offices. When you receive your provisional licence back from the DVLC it allows you to drive a car or small van under the supervision of anyone holding a full driving licence. You must first sign that licence in ink (remember the same applies to your full licence when you get it).

3. You must have eyesight sufficiently good for normal driving. If you need spectacles or contact lenses for that, you must wear them to comply with the law. The minimum legal requirement is to be able to read a number plate from 75 feet (22.9 metres) for the slightly taller style of number plate letters, or 67 feet (20.4 metres) for the shorter letters. You will be asked to prove your eyesight thus, at the beginning of your Driving Test. So try it soon before you get behind the wheel. Give yourself time to go to your optician should you need to. If corrected vision will improve matters, you should have it even if you can reach the minimum standard without. At the wheel you need the best vision you can have.

WHAT DOES THE LAW DEMAND OF YOUR CAR?

A multiplicity of laws and regulations of lesser concern affect your car but three are fundamental.

1. The car must be licensed. That tax disc must be displayed at the bottom left (nearside) corner of your front windscreen.

2. The car must be insured specifically for *you* to drive it. You must discuss the position with the person who has insured the car which you will be driving. (Note that that person isn't always the apparent owner.) Also make sure that the insurance specifically allows for the supervision of whoever will be your instructor (whether he be the insurer, the owner or neither of those). Lastly find out whether the full normal policy cover will apply. Many policies only give 3rd party cover to learners but that fact remains hidden in the "small print" until there's a problem. If you drive illegally without proper insurance cover, you can be prosecuted. In the event of an accident you could find yourself in financial ruin. So don't take chances over car insurance.

3. The car must be fit for the road. If it is over three years old it must have an MOT certificate. But beware! A certificate is not a legal guarantee of current roadworthiness. Be realistic if it's an "old banger" you want to learn on. Have it expertly checked over. Whatever the car, if you become concerned about its roadworthiness in any respect, have it taken to a garage.

The six laws regulating drivers and their cars which I have just described can be found at the back of your Highway Code within a section headed 'The Law's Demands'. They are listed under the first sub-heading addressed 'To Drivers of Motor Vehicles'. While you search for them read through the whole of that section. Everything there is part of the wider motoring knowledge you ultimately need to acquire.

For your own benefit check how much you are absorbing. See if you can list the six legal requirements I have written about, and how many extra ones you remember from reading the Code. How accurate and complete your answers are will tell you how much more time you may need to spend on each part of the Code.

As we now move away from rules and legal matters, this may be a convenient moment for a break if you want one.

GETTING INTO THE CAR

There is a right way to enter the driving seat safely.

Assume your car is parked, correctly facing in the direction of the traffic, on its own side of the road, as in fig. 2. Cars A and B are passing by. Pencil a line on fig. 2 to show the route you would take to the driver's seat. Mark the most dangerous point with an X. Your fig. 2 should now look like fig. 3 on page 26.

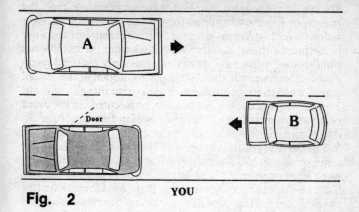

Fig. 2   YOU

X is the most dangerous point because you are vulnerable out in the road throughout the time it takes to unlock the car door. Attending to the door, you are less likely to notice what traffic may be doing around you. Whilst open, your door will be directly in the way of passing vehicles.

Therefore you mustn't simply assess the traffic before you step out. Having decided it's safe, you walk round to the driver's door without undue delay, still watching the traffic all the time. You then get in and shut the door as quickly as possible. But beware! Depending upon the width of the road, the driver of car B may attempt to squeeze through between you and car A. He should be watching you and making appropriate allowances but never count on it! Lastly see that all your other car doors are securely closed. One way you can often check is by looking in your wing mirrors.

INSTRUMENTS AND CONTROLS

Every car has a dashboard inset with sufficient instruments and switches. Other controls are positioned closely by the driver. In exotic cars, massed clusters of extra instruments can make the whole assembly resemble the flight deck of an aircraft!

You need to be able to find each of the major controls quickly *without taking your eyes off the road*. When you progress to night driving you must also be able to avoid

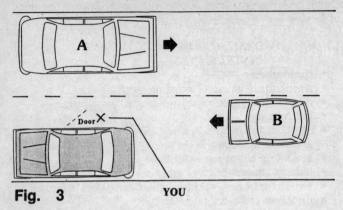

Fig. 3   YOU

fumbling when you want to work the light switches, windscreen wipers, or de-misting arrangements.

You can learn a great deal about the instruments, controls and workings of your car on your own from the driver's instruction book. (If it is missing, or you prefer to go straight to the car with your instructor, do. However, I strongly recommend time with the instruction book at some stage.) Your job is to identify where each item listed below appears in your car. Find out whether switches have to be moved up–down, or in–out, or have to be twisted. Some do all three in order to get a number of functions on the same control. See whether there is an associated tell-tale light with each switch. (If you see a warning light lit up on the dashboard you are going to need to know what it means.) Discover what the gauges show and in which direction they read.

GROUP 1 – FLOOR-MOUNTED CONTROLS

* accelerator
* brake
* clutch
* handbrake
* gear lever

The accelerator pedal is used to make the car go faster. The brake is used to slow it down. The clutch is needed when changing gear. With automatic transmission you have no

clutch pedal or gear lever. I deal with automatics at the end
of Lesson 2.

GROUP 2 – DASHBOARD CONTROLS AND INSTRUMENTS

* speedometer
* temperature gauge or warning light
* oil pressure gauge or warning light
* petrol gauge
* switches for headlamps and side lights (though these are often in Group 3, see below)
* headlamp beam reminder light
* battery charge meter or warning light
* switch for hazard warning lights (sometimes in Group 3)
* direction indicator repeater lights
* rear fog lamp switch and reminder light
* heater and demister controls
* rear window heater switch and reminder light

If heater controls seem complex, the main thing you must
know is how to maximise windscreen de-mist if rain or snow
comes on suddenly.

If your car has a manual choke, the choke lever will also
operate from on or near the dashboard.

GROUP 3 – STEERING COLUMN STALK-TYPE CONTROLS

* side lights and headlamps on/off switch (where not dashboard-mounted)
  * headlamp dipswitch and flasher control combined with:
  * direction indicator switch
* windscreen wash/wipe switches
* horn switch (either on a stalk – perhaps one of those above, or there will be a specific sector in the middle of the steering wheel to press)

You should also find the key-operated ignition switch
located on the side of the steering column, although some
cars have it on the dashboard – mostly older cars which do
not have a steering lock integral with the key operation.

Note how the direction indicator switch is often mounted on the same stalk as the headlamp flasher switch. If you interfere with this on the road without understanding, you can easily be flashing your headlamps as well as indicating your turning intentions. As such flashing may be taken as a message, this can have disastrous results. See page 113.

If you have taken the trouble to gain advance knowledge from the instruction handbook I hope you will be able suitably to impress your instructor when you call him to go out to the car, by showing HIM everything 'in situ' including details of how each item is worked. Otherwise of course he will have to show you. In the car you need to go through all three groups trying things out as you go. Your instructor can make sure you don't use any control or switch that you shouldn't whilst stationary and explain additional kit your car may have beyond the items listed here. Getting out to the car makes a break before you go on to study the transmission system.

TRANSMISSION

Your car will either have a MANUALLY operated gearbox or an AUTOMATIC one. A manual system will have a gear lever and a clutch pedal. An automatic will have no clutch pedal and it will have a selector arm in place of the gear lever. If you pass your Test on a car with automatic gears, you only become licensed to drive such vehicles, whereas those who pass with manual gears can then drive both types. Since most learners go for the fuller licence the lessons here are based on manual gears. If you do learn with automatic gears it should be obvious as you come to them which sections you can by-pass. Specific details of driving with automatic gears are at the end of Lesson 2.

The components which connect an ENGINE to the ROADWHEELS are collectively called the TRANSMIS-SION SYSTEM. They include the gearbox. If you have ridden a bicycle, you will be familiar with the effects of gears. They intervene between the engine (or pedaller) and the roadwheels to change their relative speeds. For the same engine speed the roadwheels can go fast for a motorway or slowly uphill. Inside the gearbox are cogs – toothed wheels meshed together. When you change gear you are altering

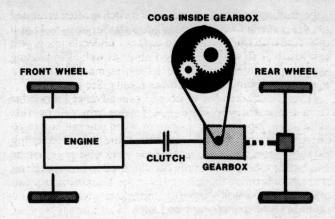

PLAN VIEW OF THE TRANSMISSION SYSTEM

Fig.   4

their meshing arrangements. To do this while the engine and gearbox are connected together, would damage the gear teeth. You therefore disconnect the two each time you change gear. This is not as drastic as it sounds. You do it with the clutch.

The clutch consists of two plates normally held locked together by springs. Pressing down the clutch pedal moves these plates apart, thereby separating the engine on the one side from the gearbox on the other, as shown in section in fig. 4. Some cars have rear-wheel drive (as in this figure), some front-wheel drive, and some four-wheel drive but the clutch principle is the same for all.

Before we continue to investigate the clutch, notice how the main components of the transmission system seen in fig. 4 connect to the major controls and instruments as shown by fig. 5.

CLUTCH PEDAL

When you press down the clutch pedal only a small band of the pedal's travel actually moves the clutch plates apart to separate the gearbox from the engine. Fig. 6 shows a side elevation of the pedal. At A, with your foot OFF the pedal,

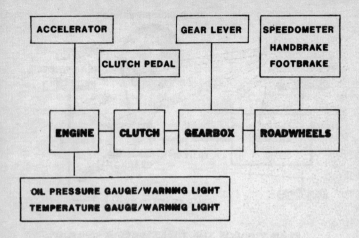

Fig. 5   THE TRANSMISSION SYSTEM

the two plates are locked together under pressure from the clutch springs. The engine is connected to the gearbox as is normal for driving along in an appropriate gear.

The clutch pedal is spring-loaded and will always return to A when you remove your foot. When you are not using the clutch, position your foot clear of the pedal. A foot resting on it will cause rapid wear.

When the clutch pedal is pressed down as far as B, the clutch plates just begin to separate. The engine plate still turns the gearbox plate but with some slipping between the two. A further small downward movement of the pedal forces them apart completely. Position B is known as the biting point. When you hold the clutch at B, you are said to be "slipping the clutch".

At C the pedal is pressed comfortably beyond the biting point. The plates are by then separated fully; the gearbox is disconnected from the engine and a gear change can be made.

Before you move a car from rest you press the clutch pedal down as far as C to separate the plates. You only press it as far as C; there's no need for it to reach the floor. You next select 1st gear and then raise the clutch pedal to B, the point

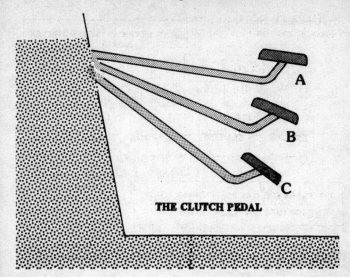

THE CLUTCH PEDAL

Fig. 6

at which the plates begin to bite. (Note how you approach the biting point from below.) You hold the clutch there while you check round for safety. Once safe, you move away by letting off the handbrake and releasing the remaining clutch pedal back to A in one controlled movement.

Gear changes on the move simply require the clutch pedal pushed down to C while the next gear is selected, and for it to be returned smoothly to A straightaway.

Use of the clutch is simplified above for the purposes of this lesson. I give the full co-ordinated routine when you first use it in practice.

The brief quiz your instructor promised, now follows.

PLEASE RETURN BOOK TO INSTRUCTOR

HIGHWAY CODEBREAKER

Informal Quiz to be given by instructor.

1. Q. What proportion of *all* road users involved in accidents are the worse for drink – beyond the legal limit for drivers?
    A. About one third.

2. Q. If you suffer from or develop a long term health condition likely to affect your driving, what must you do?
    A. Inform the driving licence authority.

3. Q. Name six mechanical car parts the law insists are in working order before you drive.
    A. Brakes, steering, windscreen wipers and washers, horn, speedometer.

4. Q. Does a vehicle insurance automatically cover a learner to drive it?
    A. Not necessarily. See page 23.

5. Q. At what age must a vehicle have an MOT certificate?
    A. Three years – renewable annually thereafter.

6. Q. What precautions should you take if you are affected by drugs or illness or tiredness?
    A. You should not drive. If you are driving STOP as soon as possible.

7. Q. Can your driving be affected after drinking below the amount the legal limit allows?
    A. Yes – well below.

8. Q. If you do not have rear seat belts, what can you do to improve the safety of a child in the car?
    A. Seat him in the front wearing an adult seat belt with a proper booster cushion.

9. Q. Whose responsibility is it for a front seat passenger to wear a seat belt?

   A. For children under 14 – the driver's. For adults – their own. It's their affair if they want to break the law but the Highway Code asks the driver to make sure they understand how to use their belt nevertheless.

10. Q. Name an extra precaution to take when children are in the back seat.

    A. Secure the child safety locks if fitted.

11. Q. Can you mount your 'L' plates in the corners of the front or back windows?

    A. No. Your windows must be kept clear of obstructions. That makes hanging dollies and paraphernalia illegal too!

12. Q. What is the purpose of the clutch?

    A. It is used to connect – or disconnect – the engine and the gearbox while you start off or change gear.

ASSESSMENT

After the quiz, review progress against the objectives of the lesson. Answer questions and give additional explanations needed. If some of the Highway Code learning is shaky, or perhaps the existence of a vital warning light wasn't noticed, try not to make an inquisition of it. Simply record on your Progress Chart whatever needs revision and say that you will expect it to be up to scratch in due course. When you set the time for Lesson 2 remember 'L' plates are going to be required.

LESSON 2

FIRST STEPS WITH CLUTCH AND GEARS

OBJECTIVES

For your learner to be able to:-
1. Demonstrate the sequence of actions for changing gear –*without looking down*.
2. Establish his routine "cockpit" safety drill before starting the engine.
3. Start the engine, select 1st gear and find the clutch biting point.

AUTOMATIC TRANSMISSION

At the end of this lesson you will find specific notes on this. Apart from the obvious differences involved the rest of the lesson is intended for teaching in the same way to all.

LOCATION and DURATION

Together in the car – which will not move – for about three quarters of an hour. 'L' plates must now be fitted.

BRIEFING

Put your learner at ease by explaining the objectives and that the car will not move in this lesson. Tell him that target objective 3 has been set for this lesson because it is a prerequisite of learning to move off smoothly – which will be the main target of Lesson 3. From your Progress Chart (fig. 1) run over doubtful areas arising from Lesson 1. Make sure your trainee has now grasped things you asked him to look through again. Avoid prompting over detail. You want to hear from him to be certain what *he* understands.

LESSON PLAN

STAGE 1 – Have your learner sitting in the driving seat. Demonstrate how to move the seat back and forth until it is in the best position. (This is usually easiest if you squat outside his open door.) Emphasise the locking mechanism to ensure the seat cannot move unexpectedly. Now adjust the angle of the seatback and again show how that has to be locked. Your learner should be comfortable, head held high, arms and knees about half bent, able to reach the steering wheel easily as in fig. 7. He must also be able to press hard on the brake pedal without completely straightening his right leg. His left foot needs to be able to work the clutch pedal with the heel pivoted on the floor, unless that proves impossible.

Fig. 7

STAGE 2 – With yourself back in the car and all doors securely shut, demonstrate how to adjust all the mirrors. The interior mirror should be set so that the top edge lines up with the top of the rear window, and the right-hand edge aligns with the right-hand edge of the rear window. Show how the night dazzle facility works if it has one. When the external mirrors are correctly set, the tops of the outside back passenger door handles will just be visible in the bottom inside corners of the respective mirrors. This will maximise the driver's view of the blind areas fanning out rearwards behind each side of the car. He should gain a long, clear sighting of anyone overtaking, or moving up on the inside. Having set them, emphasise how blind spots *still remain*. To drive this point home, get out and hide in them. Before getting out for this or perhaps for setting an external mirror to start with, take the opportunity to warn about your responsibility to see that opening your door will be safe. Explain how here, for your passenger door, you look behind especially for pedestrians such as joggers, and for pavement cyclists.

STAGE 3 – Ensure both of you have fastened your seat belts.

STAGE 4 – Instruct your pupil how to hold the steering wheel in the ten-to-two position as in fig. 8.

HOLDING THE STEERING WHEEL

Fig. 8

STAGE 5 – Instruct your learner to press the clutch pedal down with his left foot to beyond the biting point. Show him how far that is, compared with pushing it right to the floor. While he keeps it down, demonstrate moving the gear lever in sequence through the gears. Now let him practise the sequence. Insist he does it without looking down. Once he can find his way up and down the forward gears sequence (including 5th gear if there is one), instruct him to select his own choice of gears individually at random – always finding neutral for a moment, between selections. If he hasn't already found it, next show him reverse.

STAGE 6 – Introduce the USE of the clutch while changing gear. Explain the sequence:

    CLUTCH DOWN
    GEAR CHANGE
    CLUTCH UP.

Let him continue the gear changing, adding the use of the clutch. Stop him instantly if he looks down. Remind him to rest his foot clear of the pedal between changes.

STAGE 7 – Now he's familiar with his left foot being his clutch foot, explain how it is the right foot that you always use for both the accelerator and brake and that both of them are spring-loaded just as the clutch is. Make clear that the foot is used gently – no stabbing or ramming at the pedals. Then let him practise moving his foot lightly between the two while you call out, "Speed up" and "Slow down".

STAGE 8 – Explain how clutch and accelerator are normally used in conjunction but 'in opposition', one pedal moving upwards while the other moves downwards. Get him to practise both simultaneous clutch down/accelerator up, and vice versa, a few times each.

STAGE 9 – Now get him to put together Stages 5–8 and practise synchronising the use of the three pedals and gear lever together. Tell him to move UP through the gears, taking his foot off the accelerator each time he presses the clutch down, as well as restoring some acceleration each time the clutch comes up again.

Explain that changing DOWN differs because, as you are normally slowing down, you don't accelerate after the change. He can now practise moving up and down the gears until his skill is entirely fluent.

Next he can do some more of the same joined-up practice with you calling out, "Speed up" and "Slow down" whilst he is in different gears. You can watch his footwork and comment if necessary. Finish with a few changes direct from 4th to 2nd (or 5th gear to 3rd) as they are occasionally useful.

STAGE 10 – "COCKPIT" DRILL

Explain that whenever a driver gets in he must, before anything else:-

1. CHECK ALL DOORS ARE PROPERLY SHUT.
    (His responsibility – particularly so if children are aboard.)
2. CHECK THE DRIVING SEAT ADJUSTMENT/ SECURITY.
3. FASTEN SEAT BELTS.
4. CHECK SETTING OF ALL MIRRORS.

To help instil the habit, ask your learner to review these four items again now.

STAGE 11 – ENGINE START-UP

Demonstrate each point yourself (from the passenger seat) before your learner tries the sequence.

1. CHECK HANDBRAKE ON SECURELY.
    (Pause here to demonstrate use of the handbrake. Ask your pupil to keep his foot on the footbrake while you do so. Show use of the ratchet release button with the thumb and how you always have to pull the handbrake on a fraction more before you can release it. Also show the correct firmness with which the handbrake is applied – enough, without overdoing it. Point out that to save wear and tear on the ratchet, you shouldn't let it "click" all the way up on

application; you should hold the button in and only release it to hold the lever once the handbrake is set. Check your pupil still has his foot firmly on the footbrake. Then let him try the handbrake a few times. Make sure he leaves it on before you continue with 2.)

2. CHECK GEAR LEVER FOR NEUTRAL.
3. APPLY CHOKE IF APPLICABLE.
   (This book deals with the choke later, so you can pass on with the briefest of explanations.)
4. TURN IGNITION STARTER KEY.
5. RELEASE KEY DIRECTLY ENGINE FIRES.
6. CHECK BATTERY AND OIL WARNING LIGHTS, AND PETROL GAUGE.

Switch off again for Stage 12.

STAGE 12 – To help your learner form good habits, you may like to suggest that the "COCKPIT" DRILL and ENGINE START-UP SEQUENCE are each more easily remembered as Rules of Three:-

COCKPIT DRILL:
1. DOORS   2. SEATS AND BELTS   3. MIRRORS

START UP:
1. HANDBRAKE   2. GEAR   3. START AND CHECK.

As a last step before a "live" trial make sure your trainee can complete both routines one after the other without fault.

STAGE 13 – Now ask him to START THE ENGINE himself. Be ready to jump at the slightest sign he might be going to forget part of the routine.

When he checks the petrol gauge explain how far the car should go on that amount of petrol and how far on a full tank, so he can learn to relate readings to distances.

If you have been using a manual choke, show your learner how to ease it in progressively. If not (but you do have a manual choke) it's a good moment to show him its correct closed (off) position.

STAGE 14 – With the engine running smoothly, have your learner gently press the accelerator. Ask him to listen to the engine note at different accelerator pressures. Do not let him race the engine for more than a moment; point out the damage that this could cause – not least to your ears! Indicate the level of engine acceleration you set prior to moving away from rest on the level.

Explain that when he is finding the clutch biting point (in the next stage) listening for a drop in the engine note is going to be one of the key ways of knowing he has found it.

STAGE 15 – Change over seats. Be ready to challenge your learner if he appears not to be going to look behind before opening his door. That fundamental habit has got to stick!

You can now demonstrate to him finding the clutch biting point, emphasising the sequence. With the engine running:-

1. CHECK HANDBRAKE FULLY ON.
2. DEPRESS CLUTCH.
3. SELECT 1ST GEAR.
4. RAISE ENGINE SPEED TO HOLD FAST IDLE.
5. SMOOTHLY RELEASE CLUTCH PEDAL UP TO BITING POINT.
   (Point out reduction in engine speed and tone when the plates begin to slip together, combined with the car's "urging-to-go" straining against the handbrake, as you reach the biting point.)

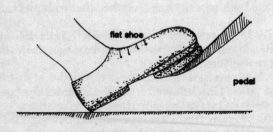

HEEL FIRMLY ON THE FLOOR

Fig. 9

6. HOLD PEDAL THERE, STEADY, FOR A MOMENT;
   THEN PRESS IT BACK DOWN.
7. RETURN GEAR LEVER TO NEUTRAL.
8. RELEASE ACCELERATOR AND CLUTCH
   PEDALS. RELAX.

During your demonstration highlight how to pivot your heel on the floor as in fig. 9. Explain that a normal flat shoe is easiest to pivot and that this is the best way to achieve the surest control. After your demonstration answer queries. If necessary repeat the demonstration or any part of it. Then change seats again.

Before your pupil carries out this sequence warn him of the dangers of overshooting the biting point in step 5, or letting the clutch pedal rise without thinking, during step 6. Explain that if that were to happen and the car to jerk forward, he must get the clutch down again quickly and simultaneously snap his right foot on to the footbrake to stop the car. (The handbrake would not necessarily be enough to hold it.) And that, from there, provided he keeps the clutch down 'til he's ready, it should be simple enough to pick up the sequence again at step 4. (If it will help, change seats once more and show him what can happen, so he sees how the quick foot reaction solves the problem.)

The possibility of a minor overshoot of the biting point making the car stall instead, also needs mentioning. Explain how the effort of getting a heavy car moving directly the biting point is passed will stop the engine unless it is taken up smoothly with sufficient power; and how to pass that point whilst leaving the handbrake inadvertently on, will be just as likely to cause a stall. Promise your learner that as the matter will be better learnt "live" you will instruct him exactly what to do next when his first stall happens – probably before the end of this lesson!

STAGE 16 – Check that your learner feels confident about the order to do everything. Then let him find the biting point himself. Be ready to remind if he forgets anything the first few times and watch for correct heel pivot technique. Let him practise finding it again and again but don't let him hold it there for more than a second or two each time. Insist throughout that he does not look down. (Note: If he has difficulty in pivoting his heel but is able to work the clutch competently mainly by use of the thigh muscle instead, there is no need to insist; let it go. Be on guard in case he accidentally releases the clutch and jams the accelerator down in panic. You must knock the gear lever into neutral in a flash.)

It is almost inevitable that he *will* stall. You must (you have promised!) be reassuring, positive and exact in instructing him on the correct recovery procedure. So list the steps as a Rule of Three to remember:-

STALLING:
1. FOOTBRAKE ON (hold car instantly) THEN HANDBRAKE
2. SELECT NEUTRAL
3. DOUBLE-CHECK HANDBRAKE/GEAR; START ENGINE.

In the confusion of a stall in traffic, that double-check will pay its way. If he stalls repeatedly during his practice, halt for a 'breather'. The strain on leg, ankle and brain can be considerable for both of you . . .

STAGE 17 – ENGINE SWITCH-OFF sequence
After your pupil has had a few successes at the eight steps of finding the biting point, explain the normal switch-off Rule of Three:-

1. HANDBRAKE ON FIRST   2. GEAR TO NEUTRAL
3. THEN IGNITION OFF

and ask him to carry it out. (During the biting point exercise the handbrake has been on but he should still check it so as to establish the right routine.)

STAGE 18 – Ask your learner to demonstrate as one whole, everything he has learned from "cockpit" drill to switch-off. Only prompt if he is about to leave something out or asks for help, or if he makes a mistake. Better still is to ask him to "teach" you as he goes.

Though it won't apply 'til driving itself starts, be warned, learners happy to end a session forget detail when they switch off, such as pulling on the handbrake . . .

ASSESSMENT

It's worthwhile drawing up, as in fig. 10, a check list of the objectives to hand to your pupil after each lesson. Explain your reasons for each assessment. Praise where he has shown real promise. Explain what will be needed where he's done less well.

LESSON ASSESSMENT

OBJECTIVE (write the objective in the space provided)	complete achievement	partial achievement	no achievement	NOTES

tick the appropriate box

Fig. 10

Agree when the next lesson will be. While this one is still fresh in mind, note on your Progress Chart (fig. 1) things you will want to recap then. The next few pages are for your learner to read before Lesson 3.

HAND BOOK BACK TO LEARNER

HOME STUDY

The law demands that you be in a position to exercise full control and command full vision all round.

That is why your instructor took such trouble showing you how to adjust and lock your seat. (My seat once broke adrift while I was doing 50 mph. It wasn't funny.) Your clothing must not interfere with full control. For example, wellington boots are inappropriate – they could risk clumsy footwork, leading to an accident; you dare not drive in muddy shoes; a lady's wedding hat mustn't obscure the interior mirror; etc., etc.

"Full vision" demands that you can see a small dog six feet in front of the bonnet, just as much as that you can see the road way out ahead. It means sitting up so that both sides of the road are kept well in view. It is from them that other traffic or pedestrians may swing across your bows. It means having all mirrors set properly. Lastly, it means mirrors and windows must be clean. Dirt on them severely restricts vision. It should be no surprise to learn that to have dirty windows is a (little-known) Offence.

When you carry out your "cockpit" drill before you drive in the next lesson, have all the above in mind. If you need to use a cushion because of your height or you need to remove unnecessary window stickers, do so. Don't imagine that it doesn't matter.

You learned only to use your left foot on the clutch and your right foot for either the brake or accelerator as in fig. 11. Using your feet as described prevents ever mistakenly using the accelerator against the brake or vice versa.

You learned to release the accelerator as your clutch goes down for a gear change. There is bound to be an occasion when you forget and the engine screams as a result. Don't

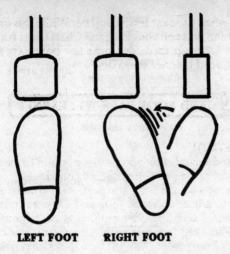

LEFT FOOT   **RIGHT FOOT**

Fig. 11

panic. Just lift your foot off the accelerator. A brief roar
from the engine won't damage it.

   Grab a scrap of paper and write down the four Rules of
Three you were introduced to in the practical start of this
lesson:- "Cockpit" Drill, Engine Start-up, Engine Switch-
off, Stalling. Any doubts or errors doing this mean you need
to go back and learn these basics by heart before Lesson 3.

CHOKE

   Even if your car has an automatic choke you need to
understand how a choke works.

   Your car runs on a mixture of petrol and air. That mixture
compressed and then ignited explodes. A continuous series
of explosions inside the engine cylinders in turn, is the force
which propels the car. The muffled burr of the engine when it
is running is the sound of those explosions. The device which
mixes the petrol and air may be a mechanical one called a
CARBURETTOR, or an electronically programmed one
known as FUEL INJECTION.

   Fig. 12 shows how the *amount* of mixture fed into the
engine is controlled by the ACCELERATOR.

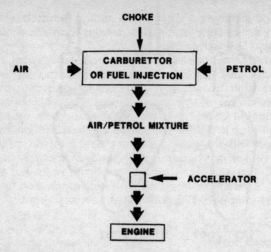

Fig.   12

For a cold start, and during its warm up, an engine needs an enriched mixture having more petrol blended with less air. The choke does the trick – simply by 'choking' off some of the normal air supply. With fuel injection, choke arrangements are automatic. With a carburettor, the choke can be manual or automatic.

A manual choke works from a pull-out knob on or near the dashboard. It is designed to stay in whatever position you set it: fully out for rich mixture; fully home for normal running; varying positions between, during warm-up. You only pull it out when starting the engine from cold. As she warms up you gradually push the knob home. You would expect to dispense with the choke within 2–3 minutes, or a mile or so of running.

A mistake even experienced drivers make is forgetting to push home a manual choke. This wastes fuel, harms the engine and may lead to the engine stalling (cutting out) once it is hot – often at a dangerous spot like a crossroads – because it is then being fed with too rich a mixture. Your car may have a choke "on" warning light, a valuable help against this error. But you can also cause the engine to stall by pushing home the choke too soon. Then the engine stops (unless you manage to "catch it" by pulling the choke out again in time) because the mixture remains too weak while the engine is still warming up.

To know the right time to push the choke home listen to the sound of the engine. If when you take your foot off the accelerator after driving a whole mile, it is still chugging with an up-and-down, fast–slow sound (as it does when first started on full choke) you are giving too much choke. Reckon to push it in in quicker stages. On the other hand, if the engine is still struggling to move the car at a normal speed after a mile, you may be pushing it in too early. Each car has its own foibles and even they change over time, as well as whenever it has a tune-up. Having an automatic choke offers the convenience of having none of this to worry about!

ENGINE STARTING TECHNIQUE

Some cars require a slight touch on the accelerator for starting when the engine is warm. Others need none. The usual cold-start rule is to use choke (automatic chokes do it for you) but no accelerator (a linkage explained in Lesson 3 pre-sets just the right small amount). Checking the maker's instruction handbook is the best way to be sure of your facts. Your instructor is sure to know any special peculiarities of your car too.

The following tips may help you become sensitive to an engine's needs. If you do have to use some accelerator for starting, take care neither to press down too far nor to squeeze the pedal up-and-down repeatedly. This is especially important when the engine doesn't start first time. Doing so can FLOOD the engine. As the word suggests, too much mixture gets sprayed into the cylinders and they cannot fire, wet with almost neat petrol.

Excessive use of a manual choke before a cold engine start can cause flooding too. If she doesn't go within a few attempts, try without choke. Once she fires, you can pull it out again if necessary.

On most cars to clear suspected flooding, you floor the accelerator, hold it there, and spin the engine on the starter for a few moments (manual choke off). Signs of trying to start will soon confirm the diagnosis. Release most of the accelerator, try again, and she normally goes. Once running, a manual choke may have to be reintroduced until she's warmed up.

In Stage 16 earlier in this lesson you learned how to recover quickly from an engine stall. Look at that Rule of Three now (page 42) and consider how you would have to adapt it if the stall was triggered by your using too much (or too little) choke. And think what you would do if you then flooded the engine, making matters worse. These things do happen. You need to be prepared.

When you turn the ignition key 'on', look for battery and oil warning lights to come on. Not until you turn the key further – against spring-loading – will you hear the starter motor burst into life. The engine should fire straightaway. Immediately it does, you must release the key. (It returns itself to 'on'.) If the engine does not fire within about five seconds, release the key. If it has still not started after half-a-dozen five-second tries, wait. Find out what the problem is before you wreck the battery with further ill-founded attempts. Starting is the toughest job the battery has to do. You can preserve its life (and increase your chances of quick starting) if you always: a) switch off everything electrical first (except if side lights have to be on at night), b) hold the clutch pedal down. (This removes clutch/gear-train drag.)

As soon as the engine starts, check that the oil pressure and battery warning lights go out straightaway. If either stays lit (or an oil gauge shows little or no reading) stop the engine. An engine without oil pressure can be ruined within a few minutes. If the battery is not being recharged you will soon get stuck.

CLUTCH WEAR

We need to slip the clutch to transfer the engine's power gradually into movement of the car, as you have learned. The biting point exercise you have done was to teach you accurately to find the precise stage of clutch pedal release that equates with maximum clutch slipping, the stage of pedal release that requires total control to prevent leapfrogging away like a scalded cat! Such learning exercises naturally wear out clutch plates more quickly than normal. Slipping causes friction. Friction equals wear. However, expensive as they are to replace, eating into the useful life of the clutch plates more hungrily while learning is an accepted cost of doing so. You learn how to minimise that clutch wear as soon as you are competent.

A set of clutch plates can last upwards of 70,000 miles, though on a driving school car they may be lucky to reach a third of that life. For this reason less scrupulous professional instructors may try to skimp clutch control teaching. Insist you are taught properly or change teachers.

HIGHWAY CODEBREAKER

Before your next lesson read the three sub-sections headed: Signs, Signals, and Moving Off, which come under THE ROAD USER ON WHEELS in the Highway Code. Then, test yourself with the brief quiz below.

QUESTIONS

1. Which five road signs show a picture of a bicycle but no other vehicle? Describe the signs and give their meanings.

2. What is the meaning of a circular red road sign with a horizontal white bar?

3. What arm signal would you give a traffic warden or policeman to show that you intend to go straight ahead?

4. Who else on the road apart from drivers give signals? What should you do when you see them?

5. Before moving off, what two checks will you make for other traffic behind?

ANSWERS

1. A black bicycle on a white background inside a red circle means – no cycling. A white bicycle on a blue circular background means – route for pedal cycles only. A black bicycle on a white background inside a red triangle means – cycle route ahead. A white bicycle on a blue oblong background means – recommended route for pedal cycles. As the previous sign but with a vertical

white line to right of the cycle means – with-flow pedal cycle lane.

    Note: a separate rule in the Code stipulates that where a cycle lane is marked by a solid line at the side of the road it is an offence to drive or park on that lane. You may cross it where there are breaks in the line but not unnecessarily.

2.   No entry.

3.   Left hand raised with palm forward. It needs to be held just above shoulder height and well forward to be seen properly.

4.   The Code mentions people in authority, motorcyclists and pedal cyclists; but anyone may have valid reason to do so and you could be foolish to ignore them. When you see a signal take necessary action promptly.

5.   (a) Use the mirrors. (b) Look over your right shoulder as a final check.

Unless you are using a car with automatic gears, move on to Lesson 3 on page 53.

HAND BOOK BACK TO INSTRUCTOR

LEARNING WITH AUTOMATIC GEARS

    Only your right foot must use the foot pedals, the accelerator and the footbrake. Your left foot should never be used. (Some drivers suggest using the left foot on the brake in combination with the right foot on the accelerator during slow manoeuvres. It is unnecessary. Response to the right foot on the accelerator is very gentle at low engine speeds, a factor inherent in the design. The danger of such a both-feet habit is that in an emergency, at speed, you might hit the accelerator and brake simultaneously.)

    The gear selector usually has the following positions:-

P (park)

    Gears in neutral. Gearbox mechanically locked so car will not move. As name implies, **P** should be selected whenever car is parked. In event of handbrake failure, car should remain safely held. Note:- usually, engine can only be started in Park, or in Neutral, discussed next. You must therefore remember that if you stall the engine you have to select **N** or **P** rapidly, before you can re-start.

N (neutral)
Engine start position. Gears are in neutral.

R (reverse)
(Move off technique same as for Drive below.)

D (drive)
You start the engine in **N** or **P**. You then apply the footbrake and select **D**. When you are ready to move away, take off the handbrake in anticipation; all that remains is to release the (foot)brake and transfer your foot to apply gentle pressure to the accelerator. The car will move off. As you apply more pressure the gearbox automatically changes up into the higher gears. Most automatics have three or four gears and the gear changes are determined by the car's road speed in relation to the load on the engine. Thus the gearbox automatically changes back down the gears as speed decreases, or if the load on the engine increases, for example, going uphill.

In theory, the handbrake should always be applied during traffic queue stops. In practice it is only really demanded when the stop is of long duration, or for other traffic or pedestrians to cross immediately in front of you, for example, when you reach the entry to a roundabout, or at a Pelican crossing or Stop sign. Otherwise you can simply remain in **D** and hold the car on the footbrake. However, you would use the handbrake more often on a wet night. You would do so whenever the glare of your brakelights staying on could be a nuisance to drivers waiting behind.

With the handbrake on, there is technically no need to return to Neutral because the handbrake should easily hold the car in Drive so long as your foot is off the accelerator and the engine no more than ticks over. However, a faulty handbrake or accelerator, or even a mix up by your feet, could lead to a lurch forward and this justifies a return to

Neutral in circumstances where that would be catastrophic, for example, if jay-walkers are squeezing between you and the car in front. It is a matter of judgment; it costs nothing and adds to safety.

L (lock)

There may be occasions (for example, long steep hills up or down) when you want to over-ride the automatic selection and keep in low gear. You select Lock. Depending upon type, there may be a Lock provision for each low gear individually, or for example, for the transmission to be held in 2nd gear or below but still changing between 1st and 2nd if required.

A separate "kick-down" feature enables you to gain a burst of speed, for example, when overtaking. You just floor the accelerator. This "instructs" the gearbox to drop down to the lowest appropriate gear for your speed at the time. Maximum acceleration, making best use of the gears, will be yours until you relax the accelerator again. If you are already going faster than "kick-down" can help you, the system simply ignores your foot.

Your instructor will know about any differences with your automatic gears as compared with these notes. All the lessons that follow are structured so that you can simply substitute automatic gear techniques appropriately as you go along.

HAND BOOK BACK TO INSTRUCTOR

LESSON 3

STARTING AND STOPPING

OBJECTIVES

For your learner to be able to:-
1. Use an indicator signal.
2. Safely move away from rest in 1st gear.
3. Change up.
4. Stop gently: a) as if in a traffic queue, b) when pulling in.
5. Demonstrate a Quick-Reaction stop in response to an unpredicted event.

DURATION and LOCATION

The ideal is 45–60 minutes out in the car. To complete the lesson there are a few pages of home study and a self-quiz for the learner.

A quiet, level road with no other traffic is needed. You could find a deserted farm track with the owner's permission, or perhaps, on a Sunday morning, an empty road on a trading estate. Remember 'L' plates. Cover or remove them except when your learner takes the wheel.

YOUR LOOK OUT!

From the first moment your learner makes the car move, you must be watching other traffic just as if you were driving.

He will be concentrating upon learning many new skills at once. You can guarantee that he will not always see potential danger. Be prepared to issue timely warnings.

Suppose, as your learner is ready to bring the clutch up to the biting point, an early-morning stroller appears in front of the car, walking his dog *off* the lead, and you realise that your learner has not noticed. You mustn't hesitate to say, "Hold your feet where they are; I want you to tell me why you must not move away yet." I gave other examples under Dangerous Mistakes, page 11.

An extra mirror can be an advantage, but never be tempted to rely on that alone. Fit it away from anywhere it could give you a nasty bump in an Emergency Stop.

BRIEFING

Before the lesson starts, refer on your Progress Chart to any failings in earlier lessons. Make sure that any difficulties have now been clarified in your learner's mind. Try not to blurt out answers. (It's easily done!) Instead, ask questions that draw proof from him that he now knows what was meant.

Run through the lesson objectives and then tell your pupil:-

1.   You will drive to a quiet traffic-free road before he takes the wheel for the first time for a short distance. Once he is in charge you will continue keeping a good look-out and will give him ample warning if you think he has failed to notice other traffic. Despite that back-up, YOU EXPECT HIM TO SEE OTHER ROAD USERS IN GOOD TIME. Your presence doesn't alter the fact that it is **HIS** responsibility.

2.   During the lesson you will always demonstrate before you ask him to try.

3.   Explain that you teach a Quick-Reaction stop on the first drive because no one can know how soon a learner may encounter a sudden danger.

4.   If the roads are wet you will leave the Quick-Reaction stop for another day; however, as the practical ground-work of this lesson is so important, you are likely to want to repeat this session anyway.

LESSON PLAN

INSTRUCTOR'S DEMONSTRATION

STAGE 1 – Stop the car at the side of the road at the chosen location. Switch off the engine so that you can then recap on Lesson 1 by carrying out "cockpit" and engine start-up drills, commenting on the key points.

STAGE 2 – Engine running again, demonstrate how to move away safely. Explain each step in sequence.

GET READY:
- PUT BOTH HANDS ON STEERING WHEEL.
  Remind how to hold it as in fig. 8. Emphasise that you must have *both hands on the wheel* except when using the handbrake, changing gear, giving an arm signal, or having to operate a switch. But that whatever you need to operate or do, both hands must *never* leave the wheel *at the same time*. Check your learner knows which way to turn the wheel to steer either way.
- LOOK OUT FOR TRAFFIC AND PEDESTRIANS, ahead, all round and in the mirrors.
- WHEN SAFE . . .
- PUSH CLUTCH PEDAL DOWN AND SELECT 1ST GEAR.
- RETURN LEFT HAND TO STEERING WHEEL.
- RAISE ENGINE SPEED TO FAST IDLE.
- RAISE CLUTCH SMOOTHLY TO BITING POINT.
  Remind to pivot left heel on floor.
- HOLD CLUTCH AND ACCELERATOR STEADY AT BITING POINT.
- RELEASE HANDBRAKE.
- RETURN LEFT HAND TO STEERING WHEEL.
  The car should be standing still, held at the self-same biting point your learner reached himself in the last lesson. In getting there this time, we have added the refinements of safety required in case of traffic.
  Now show your learner how – with no change of the accelerator position – releasing the clutch by the

smallest fraction makes the car begin to move. Immediately it moves, show how pushing the clutch back down *that same fraction* – but no more – makes it stop.

Explain that this tiny downward clutch adjustment is all you do to stop it if the car creeps forward when you first release the handbrake. If on a slope it rolls back instead, it shows a touch more power is needed to hold against the hill; in that case, raising the clutch that fraction will do the trick.

The prior setting of the accelerator is NOT altered. IT IS THE CLUTCH THAT GIVES CONTROL. (Note: the unnecessary trouble many learners have on the Hill start should never occur if this stage is well taught.)
- HOLD THE CAR STILL, HANDBRAKE OFF, balanced at the biting point while you look all round again. Then . . .

SIGNAL:
- SET RIGHT HAND INDICATOR.
 Show how your hand need not leave the wheel to do it.

LOOK BEHIND:
- CHECK ALL MIRRORS.
- TURN YOUR HEAD AND LOOK OVER YOUR RIGHT SHOULDER.
 Explain that this physical look before moving away from the kerbside is a Test requirement. You must be certain no one, especially a cyclist, is hidden in the mirrors' blind spots. If you see a succession of cars or perhaps a dumper truck coming, which means you can't go for a few moments, explain how you must cancel your indicator, pull on the handbrake, return to neutral and release the clutch. And then when the traffic is about to cease, begin the *GET READY* step again.

Once the road is clear behind . . .

LOOK AHEAD:
- NEVER pull away forwards while still looking back-

wards; you can tell your trainee that many a learner has crashed doing that!

MOVE AWAY:
- SMOOTHLY RELEASE REMAINING CLUTCH AND GENTLY INCREASE ENGINE SPEED.

  Point out that only a smooth, controlled release of the clutch, as it first rises above the biting point, will achieve a smooth transfer of power from engine to roadwheels. Once the clutch is well past the biting point and the clutch plates are no longer slipping, the remaining clutch pedal movement can be released quickly. Show how your foot must immediately be 'parked' clear of the clutch pedal, though ready for future use.
- STEER GENTLY OUT FROM THE EDGE.
- CANCEL INDICATOR.

  Emphasise this needs to be made a habit because so slight a steering movement will not trigger the automatic indicator cancelling device.

STAGE 3 – Once out from the edge on the move, discuss with your learner the distances you are leaving from the kerb. He needs to begin absorbing the relationship between different road widths and speeds, and how far out to be.

Change up to 2nd gear making sure he watches the sequence and is reminded how your right foot returns to press the accelerator afterwards because you are still increasing speed, while your left foot is once more 'parked' straightaway clear of the clutch.

STAGE 4 – Drive a short way in 2nd, before demonstrating a gentle stop such as stop/start traffic conditions might require. Comment on every action, however small, so that your pupil becomes aware of it.

PREPARE:
- CHECK MIRRORS.

  Explain that the brake lights (which come on when you first touch the pedal) will scarcely warn a motorist who is too close behind if you stop unnecessarily quickly. Emergencies apart, one reason you always stop gently is so that people have time to see your brake lights. In emergency, the fellow "glued" to your tail may or may not manage to stop, but that mustn't be allowed to affect your stopping as fast as you know how. Mention that with ordinary stops there are times, which you will consider together later, when an arm signal helps.

SLOW DOWN:
  – RELEASE ACCELERATOR.
  – PRESS BRAKE SOFTLY.
  – PRESS CLUTCH DOWN WHEN ALMOST STOPPED.

STOP:
  – KEEP GENTLE PRESSURE ON BRAKE UNTIL STOPPED, AND . . .
  – HANDBRAKE ON, AND . . .
  – NEUTRAL SELECTED. THEN . . .
  – RELEASE FOOT PEDALS.

STAGE 5 – *PREPARE STRAIGHTAWAY TO MOVE ON.*
Explain that you cannot sit in the middle of a road idly chatting! Move on again, this time having told your learner you are shortly going to pull in to the side.

As you go through Stages 2 to 4 again, you need only highlight the differences. Thus:

STAGE 2 – *GET READY:* – no right signal – no need for over-shoulder look behind – (Point out that if someone has appeared there already and is waiting for you, you go as soon as safely possible; if they are clearly going to pass, you wait; but if they can't pass anyway because of oncoming traffic, then you get on.)

STAGE 3 – maintain distance from kerb already established.

STAGE 4 – *PREPARE TO PULL IN:* – choose a spot where you won't cause an obstruction – this time make a left indicator signal after mirrors check – steer gently back towards kerbside as you slow down – stop parallel to and within 6–9″ (15–23cm) of kerb – cancel indicator before setting handbrake, etc.

Switch off the engine and take a pause to answer questions your learner needs to understand. See if he noticed how little steering wheel movement was needed during the whole exercise. (Mention that correct steering is one subject of the home study later this lesson.)

CHECK ON LEARNING

Go through Stages 1 to 5 once again "live", but this time with YOUR TRAINEE TALKING YOU through them. Do not carry out any action until he has told you what to do and how to do it. You cannot do anything unsafe, so if he makes a mistake you must hold back while you ask him why that instruction was wrong. If he happens to say "move off" without noticing someone in the way, this exercise pays off even better! Make HIM do the looking (as well as you!) and keep you informed of (a) *where* your eyes should be roving (including the mirrors) and (b) anything he has seen which you may have yet to see.

You may need to repeat some or all of the stages several times before being convinced your pupil is ready to try the sequence at the wheel. Then pull in safely, switch off and change seats.

LEARNER'S PRACTICE

Before your learner begins, re-emphasise that he must NEVER LOOK DOWN.

Ask him to use his feet now and pretend to be stopping the car. This is important. Learners sometimes panic when the car is first moving. You want to be sure that his feet will find the right pedals.

Explain how braking action should always begin gently, and gradually build up as required. As the car rolls to a stop, you ease the brake pressure and just before it finally stops, you press down the clutch. You learn to co-ordinate these actions smoothly so that the car comes to rest without any jerk.

Agree between you that from now on in all the lessons, if you ask him to stop he must do so straightaway without question.

Now let your pupil start the car and carry out the five stages you have both worked on.

Just as you did, get him to pause at the moment he releases the handbrake. He can then discover for himself the tiny extent of upward clutch movement needed to make the car begin to move, and that how to stop it is simply a matter of pressing the clutch down again that same amount.

If he makes a serious mistake take him back to Stage 1. It is unlikely he will complete the exercise cleanly to start with. So you can practise the sequence numerous times but watch for tiredness or frustration. Call for a break if you spot either and try to make sure your trainee doesn't expect too much of himself. No one ever hits perfection on their first day out.

QUICK-REACTION STOP

Once he can move off, get up to 2nd gear and then stop, all reasonably well, change over seats to introduce a Quick-Reaction Stop – unless it is raining. If it is, leave this for a repeat session on a dry road. Explain that you will pretend someone has walked in front of the car and call out "STOP!". You will then stop – concentrating on SNAPPING THE BRAKE ON RAPIDLY, MORE FIRMLY THAN USUAL BUT WITHOUT EXCESSIVE FORCE and KEEPING THE STEERING FIRMLY STRAIGHT WITH BOTH HANDS. Because speed will be very low anyway, you will be putting the clutch down straightaway with the brake. As explained in Stage 5 earlier, you will then move on again without delay, before deciding to pull in safely or whatever. Mention that this is *not* a full Emergency Stop but one from a comfortably slow speed intended to tune up reactions ready for Emergency Stops to be learned before driving in busy traffic.

Demonstrate the Stop a couple of times from under 20 mph. (Don't forget traffic behind . . .) Then swap seats again. After arranging that you will call out "STOP!" having yourself CHECKED ALL ROUND beforehand, ask your learner to move off and get up to about 15 mph in 2nd gear. Explain that all he must do is react fast, stopping quickly in a straight line WITHOUT jamming hard on the brake, and remembering to put his clutch down. After the Stop, remind him (if necessary) to move off again without delay.

Three or four tries should be enough to establish swift feet. Repeat the exercise during the next few lessons to render the response "instinctive". The full Emergency Stop is at the beginning of Lesson 10.

ASSESSMENT

By now your learner has probably done enough. *YOU* should drive home. At home, present your pupil with a check list as you did before, based on fig. 10. Take the time to analyse with him how well (or poorly) he achieved each objective. Where he's gone wrong, pin-point the reasons together if you can so that he can be thinking about them before the next drive. Make notes on your Progress Chart to remind you to return to important problems at appropriate times.

Your assessment now will indicate your next move. If you assess any objective as 'partial achievement' or 'no achievement' you will have to repeat at least that part. You may have to judge a repeat necessary even where you have been able to mark 'complete achievement', if you have done so against nearly every item. Such a learner would be showing runaway progress unless he had had prior experience. It would be wise to see that he fares equally well at a second helping before heading for Lesson 5, the next one in the car. Assuming you decide to repeat the lesson, or parts of it, reassure your learner that he only needs more time and practice on this stage (as do 99% of all learners); it doesn't mean he's a failure!

HAND BOOK TO LEARNER

HOME STUDY

MORE CHOKE FACTS

Whether you have a manual or an automatic choke it will have a linkage to the accelerator. When you pull out a manual choke the first quarter inch of knob movement acts on the accelerator to pre-set a faster engine tick-over speed.

The remaining movement available alters the petrol/air mix under your control, depending how much you have the knob pulled out, as described earlier. An automatic choke achieves the required fast idle and a perfect mixture, untouched by human hand!

The purpose of increasing the engine idle speed is to help prevent stalling. On a cold morning, that fast idle may mean that in the last yards before stopping, you need to brake or put the clutch down a little earlier than usual. Your instructor will almost certainly hand you a car with a warmed-up engine in the first few lessons but later on you must learn to cope with this minor added complication as well as using a manual choke if you have one.

STEERING

You should hold the steering wheel gently without letting it slip, not tightly. A rock-hard grasp is tiring and unnecessary. If you ever watch a black and white 1950's 'B' movie you may spot the hero hanging on to the wheel of his car like grim death and constantly swinging the car from side to side. That is NOT the right way.

On a clear straight road your hands scarcely need to move. On a gentle curve, movement should be minimal. Only a sharp bend or a turning require pronounced steering action. In the process *your hands must never cross*. You move the wheel with one hand while sliding it through the fingers of the other.

To clarify what I mean, find a circular object – as much like a steering wheel as possible. A large saucepan lid will do but a small child's hoop is better. Hold it with your hands at ten o'clock and two o'clock. To turn right, grip harder with your right hand and loosen the left enough for your "wheel" to slip through. Then move both hands downward, your right hand pulling, your left allowing the wheel to pass up through the fingers. When your hands get down near five and seven o'clock, tighten your left hand grip and relax your right hand. Your left hand now pushes the wheel up while it slips down through the fingers of the right hand which also moves up.

In the car you simply repeat this action 'til you reach the amount of steering required (or it is turned as far as it will go). As neither hand leaves the wheel you retain full control throughout. As you leave the turn you have to straighten up again. You simply reverse the movements so that the wheel turns the other way – exactly as would be required for turning left.

As you repeat the two steps in turn, fluency in alternating the use of each hand top and bottom is the key to the swift steering movements needed during slow speed manoeuvring. Go back to your simulated wheel and try left and right turns now, with three-to-four pairs of movements in quick succession, to represent a turn in one direction, followed at once by the opposite movements to equate with straightening up.

In the car 'for real', self-centering helps the wheel return straight ahead. Let it help but do not let go! Retain control with both hands staying on the wheel. Relax your grip enough for the self-centering to do its work but don't rely on it alone. Apart from minor amounts of steering, you will always need the properly executed movements just described to straighten up quickly and reliably.

ARM SIGNALS

Like indicator signals, arm signals express merely your intention. They do not create permission to do it. You must still stick to the rules which govern priorities on the road. Nevertheless, you will meet drivers who just signal and go as if that were enough. Be warned!

To return to arm signals, have a look at them in your Highway Code; both the ones you might give for the benefit of other road users and those you might direct at a traffic controller. On the Test your examiner will like to see you use the signal meaning "I intend to slow down or stop", at appropriate times. He will not prompt so you must learn to use the signal yourself. He will not usually expect you to use the other arm signals during the driving part of your Test although he may specifically ask you to use the signals meaning "I intend to turn to the right/left", during a short part of it. At the end when he asks questions on the Highway Code he may ask you to demonstrate arm signals you haven't had to use.

BRAKES

Your car has two separate braking systems: a mechanical handbrake connected to one pair of wheels only and a hydraulic footbrake working on all four wheels. You use the footbrake to slow or stop. The handbrake is only to hold the car at rest. Think of it as a parking brake, not one intended for slowing the car.

HIGHWAY CODEBREAKER

Test yourself on this short quiz:-

QUESTIONS

1. Which arm signal indicates to another road user that you intend to slow down or stop?
2. What light signal would you use to indicate that you intend to slow down or stop?
3. Which triangular warning road sign is also an instruction which must be obeyed by law?
4. What is the meaning of the red bordered circular road sign on a plain white background?
5. Does any speed restriction apply to learners?
6. Where is the safest place for a young child to travel in a car?

ANSWERS

1. Right arm moved up and down fully extended through open side window.
2. Your brake lights come on automatically the instant you touch the brake pedal. To give an early warning it is sometimes useful to dab the pedal lightly a little in advance of beginning to reduce speed.
3. Give way.
4. No vehicles.
5. No. However, except where lower limits are in force, you should feel confident in later lessons to drive up to 45 or 50 mph. That will be enough for your level of experience until well after you pass your Test.
6. The rear seat, wearing an approved child restraint appropriate to the child's age.

ADDITIONAL PRACTICE

Lesson 4 is devoted to Rules of the Road and various aspects of a car and driving which you must understand before you start to drive around and about.

Before you take the driving seat in Lesson 5 you will be even better prepared if you can polish up on the five objectives of this lesson. Ask your instructor. He will probably suggest a repeat lesson anyway, unless you have been exceptionally quick to learn or you already possess the required skills. The lesson was designed to develop EYE–HAND–FOOT co-ordination and the stage when this becomes instinctive represents a big jump forward.

Nearly every learner needs more than one go at some or all of the lesson before this happens.

Some mock practice can help too if you have the chance to sit in the car on your own to do it. BE WARNED! You must NOT practise any objective "live" without your instructor, and your car must be parked in a safe place OFF THE PUBLIC ROAD. Otherwise you could run foul of the law.

You can use the gear lever, the foot pedals, the indicator switch and so on but you must pretend so far as the handbrake and starting the engine are concerned. On no account release the handbrake. "Steer" by all means but don't actually turn the wheel, which puts abnormal strain on the steering parts when the car is stationary. Do not even consider having the ignition key in the car to tempt you. Within these constraints, you can work through the five objectives, filling in the "live" aspects with imagination. Practise synchronising foot pedals and gear lever; familiarise yourself with all controls. Have a crafty look at your instructor's lesson plan first (for this lesson only!) to see just what he would be looking out for.

Even if you can't sit in the car, you can improvise. Sit in a pretend driving seat. Picture the controls around you and use your simulated steering wheel again. Think of your feet poised at the pedals and practise away!

Lesson 4 is planned so that you can take it at your own pace until your instructor needs to step in with questions at the end. So as well as your additional practice you can be getting on with it straightaway.

LESSON 4

GETTING READY FOR THE ROAD

A lesson for home study followed with a quiz by the instructor

OBJECTIVES

For you to:-

1. Know the basic Rules of the Road.
2. Understand further principal legal obligations of a driver.
3. Recognise traffic signals, signs and road markings.
4. Know when and why you change gear.
5. Be able to carry out a roadworthiness Weekly Check.

DURATION and LOCATION

If your instructor can be around during this lesson he can answer any queries as they arise as well as give you the short test at the end. However, if you press on before he is available, note down your questions to chat over later. For the Weekly Check you need him to show you things "live", so that would also have to be delayed until he is there.

You need peace and quiet for the reading. It will take up to two hours if you attack it in one go with a couple of stops for coffee but it can just as readily be spread over shorter periods on different days.

There is no substitute for learning the contents of this lesson at this stage. Without meeting the first four objectives above, it would be unsafe to try and jump, ill-prepared, to driving the short route in Lesson 5.

But first let's look at Objective 5, a driver's responsibilities for ensuring his car is roadworthy.

Both the law and the Highway Code require a car to be roadworthy. The good driver checks everything in the list below at least once a week. He also makes sure the car is serviced at manufacturer recommended intervals. It is a policy which should keep all significant items in A1 order and reveal serious faults at the earliest moment.

WEEKLY CHECK

TYRES	– Check pressures and tread wear. Look for bulges or cuts in both inner and outer walls of each tyre.
ALL LIGHTS	– Clean lenses. Check bulbs work.
WINDOWS AND MIRRORS	– Should be spotless.
ENGINE OIL	– Check dipstick; top up if necessary.
COOLANT	– Check level in transparent header or expansion tank by eye. Refer to car handbook *before* topping up. NEVER touch radiator or any cap when hot. (In old cars no external check is possible. The radiator cap has to be removed instead, *when cold*.)
BRAKE FLUID	– Check level in reservoir. If level below minimum seek expert advice before driving.
WINDSCREEN WASHER	– Top up reservoir (rear wash/wipe may have a separate bottle). In freezing weather windscreen anti-freeze additive is essential.
BATTERY	– Check electrolyte level unless sealed for life.
GENERAL LOOK ROUND	– Check for damage, loose fittings, leakages; inspect thoroughly underneath car.

Note: Oil leaking from the engine, apart from being a hazard to other road users, can mean an expensive fault; coolant loss can also land you with a hefty bill. Neither dare be ignored, so don't drive before seeking expert help. Look for anything loose, such as the exhaust pipe or any badly rusted bodywork. They must be dealt with before the car is driven. Objects of this sort falling in the road cause serious accidents and injury. You risk being held responsible for any such harm as well as a fine for driving an unroadworthy vehicle.

A good way to learn to carry out a Weekly Check is to help your instructor next time he does it. The best place is a petrol station forecourt where air, oil, etc. are readily to hand. If you prefer to go through them together at home, any topping up can always be done next time the car is driven.

Although the Test expects very little in the way of mechanical knowledge, a good driver tries, beyond Weekly Checks and having the car serviced, to gain a reasonable understanding of which parts of a car are subject to wear and need adjustment or replacement from time to time. He doesn't just rely for roadworthiness on an MOT Test pass. That is only required by law once a year on cars three years of age and older and it is not a guarantee.

He keeps alert for dangerous faults developing – as they do – at any time. Your instructor and knowledgeable friends can help you gain sound mechanical insight if it's not already your forte.

TYRE LAW

This is subject to surprisingly frequent change. Tyre dealers are required to display the latest regulations on their premises, so a visit to a dealer can confirm current law as well as provide a chance to look at some tyres and see how various terms used are defined.

Basic legal requirements, including the spare tyre, are:-
1. There must be no bald patches in the tread.
2. There must be no bulges or slits in inner or outer side walls.
3. Structural cords embedded inside the rubber must not be exposed or affected by deep cuts.
4. At least 1 mm depth of tread must continue all round the tyre for not less than three quarters of the way in one band across the tread width at any point.

5. Cross-ply and radial-ply tyres should not normally be used on the same vehicle.
6. Tyres must be inflated to recommended pressures.

CHANGING GEARS

You use the lower gears to build up speed, for extra pulling power up hills, and faster acceleration when overtaking. They also increase control when slowing down. This is called 'engine braking'. In low gear with your foot off the accelerator, the engine provides considerable resistance against momentum. You use it driving down long steep hills to save the brakes having to work so hard.

When you slow down in traffic you use the gears partly to help braking, if that is needed. Mainly you change down for better control and so as to be in a position to speed up immediately if the traffic is able to move on. While you can easily stay in high gear and brake to a stop in traffic hold-ups, it is not good driving. Your examiner looks for greater skill. He does so because he knows how traffic varies its speed all the time in reaction to changing circumstances, and how the correct gear thus also needs to alter frequently.

GEARS FOR MOVING OFF AND ACCELERATION

You learn to judge the moment to change gear by the 'sound' and 'feel' of the engine. But to start with, until you can interpret this 'music' of the engine, a rule-of-thumb will help.

PICKING UP SPEED – LEVEL ROAD	GEAR
Rest – 10 mph	1
10 mph – 20 mph	2
20 mph – 30 mph	3
30 mph and over	4

(Ignore any 5th gear for the moment. Fifth is usually a fuel-saving cruising gear not intended for swift acceleration.)

For moving off and acceleration uphill you need to stay in the lower gears longer because of the extra effort the engine must make. Downhill the opposite applies. So much so that it is correct to move off in 2nd when starting from rest downhill. A memory trick for the table of gear speeds is to put a *0* after each gear number to give the maximum speed for that gear: (1 + 0) = ten mph, etc., until over 30 mph, when you need 4th (top) gear.

Imagine a clear road. Start in 1st (bottom) gear, accelerate to roughly 10 mph and then change into 2nd. Stay in 2nd up to about 20 mph before taking 3rd to accelerate on up to 30 mph. Around 30 mph, change into top. You can then accelerate further if desired or continue at your steady speed simply by maintaining a light pressure on the accelerator.

Always work up the gears without undue delay so that you are into top gear by the time you pass 30 mph. No one expects you to rush with 'L' plates on but if you act smartly there is surprisingly little time required between gear changes.

GEARS FOR SLOWING DOWN

The first act of slowing down, whatever gear you are in, is to raise your foot from the accelerator.

To stop quickly your foot would switch directly to the brake. You might then change down to harness engine braking as well.

For the moment though, we'll concentrate on ordinary slowing or stopping where good anticipation eliminates the need for the brakes at all, except perhaps during the final yards of a stop. Imagine you are driving along a clear road at about 40 mph in top. You see a knot of traffic way ahead and *immediately* bring your foot off the accelerator. Your speed quickly drops while you continue to assess what's ahead. You soon appreciate cars ahead are moving at a crawl and that you will need to match it when you get there. Already down to about 25 mph you drop to 3rd. Engine braking quickly cuts your speed back to 15 mph or so and you take 2nd. Now well under control you let speed trickle down to the pace needed as you join behind the others. That's perfection! A touch on the brake at some stage to get your speed just as you wanted it will almost certainly have been needed as well. As explained earlier, you need to get into 2nd not only to control the slowing down but to be able to pick up speed at once if/when the people ahead do so.

Here is a table for gear changes slowing down. (Dropping to 1st, whilst still on the move, is rarely needed but I deal with it in Lesson 6.)

SLOWING DOWN – LEVEL ROAD	SPEED
4th to 3rd	25 mph
3rd to 2nd	15 mph

In ordinary traffic circumstances you need to go down through the gears when dropping speed, with the same purposefulness required in going up through the gears during acceleration.

You will soon be aware if you leave a change down too late. The gear lever will begin to shudder. This is almost certain to happen during your first few miles at the wheel and the experience will teach you when it is too late, far better than mere words in a book!

GEARS DURING STOPPING

If it is clear from the road ahead that you will HAVE to stop, for example at a STOP sign, it is acceptable to stop using the brake helped by a change down to 3rd but leaving out changing into 2nd gear. However, wherever there is the possibility that you may be able to move on without a stop, for example entering a roundabout, a change down to 2nd so that you are ready either way, is expected. Suppose you arrive second or third in line at a traffic light recently turned red. You can stay in 3rd gear and come to a gentle stop using the footbrake during the last few yards as you learned in Lesson 3.

Take your place in the queue (as in any queue) about half a car length back from the vehicle stopped in front of you. Whether you now need the handbrake on or can sidestep the full move-on routine we will consider in a moment.

On the other hand suppose you catch up the knot of traffic described earlier to find it shortly stops for no apparent reason. You stop too! But with no idea how long the delay might be, you prepare on the basis you may well move off again immediately – on the assumption that you are only going to be stopped for a second or two.

GEARS FOR MOVING OFF AGAIN

In this brief stop case, if you are facing downhill you can stay in 2nd gear with the clutch down, holding the car on the footbrake. Set off simply by transferring your right foot to the accelerator as you gently release the clutch. On level road do the same thing but change to 1st gear beforehand. If the queueing is uphill you will have to apply the handbrake and straightaway select 1st, ready to adapt into the normal move-on part of Stage 5, Lesson 3. However, if the incline is steep, you will need to know the full Hill Start routine in Lesson 6.

All too often, a "brief" stop turns out to be longer! The lights don't turn green as quickly as you hoped or whatever. After waiting anything more than say 20 seconds you must abandon that hope, bring on the handbrake, select neutral and release the clutch. It is bad driving and harmful to the car to sit in gear and/or with the clutch down, except for very short periods. An examiner would take a very poor view. When you do move ahead, you use the full move-on routine, again as in the applicable part of Stage 5, Lesson 3.

OTHER GEAR CHANGING PRINCIPLES

Our rule-of-thumb for picking up speed suggests 2nd gear from 10 to 20 mph. However, you can stay in 2nd up to about 45 mph. Similarly, 3rd can go as high as 65 mph, depending on performance. There are several reasons for making greater use of the speeds available in these intermediate gears. Acceleration is greater. For example, 30 mph to 60 mph is achieved far more quickly in 3rd than in top.

When you overtake you want to do so as quickly as possible; where relative speeds make it appropriate you therefore drop to a lower gear to maximise acceleration.

Suppose you are doing 45 mph in top when you reach a long uphill stretch. If you stay in top you will slow down. If instead you change smartly down to 3rd, with the extra power you should be able to maintain speed until the road levels out and you can change back up to top again. If the incline is really steep you will slow down even in 3rd. If you find yourself dropping below about 35 mph, change into 2nd so you can at least keep up that speed until able to change up again. Most beginners fail to change down early enough before going uphill. Speed drops down so much the engine starts to "labour", or falter, under the strain. (Your instructor can demonstrate next time he drives you.) As a result, everyone behind groans at being slowed down unnecessarily. I hope my readers will spare other drivers this agony.

Before a long steep downhill you will often see a sign urging you to engage low gear so as to take advantage of engine braking and rely less on your brakes (although you will still need them). These signs are reserved for hills steep enough for you to find the car 'running away' unless you heed the advice. Plenty of *unmarked* downhills are equally potent.

The correct thing is to curb your speed before the descent. For most such hills on trunk routes (where the majority of drivers might descend at 30–35 mph maximum) a drop down to 3rd as you bring speed in check at the top, with perhaps a touch on the brakes half-way down to help hold the car, will be the appropriate technique. The lower gear alone may suffice. However, for a progressively dropping and really steep descent you may need continuous braking and to drop down into 2nd on the way down as well.

You make the change without relaxing your footbrake pressure.

If speed has been 'running away' beyond the comfortable range of 2nd it must be curtailed by harder braking before you change. Otherwise the car could take a tremendous jolt and perhaps skid. (The same can happen if you try to engage 3rd from top at a speed higher than the maker intended for 3rd.) Your instructor must make sure that you gain plenty of experience driving on every kind of hill so that combining the gears and brakes appropriately becomes natural.

You also drive at faster speeds in a lower gear than used for initial moving away, to improve control on winding bends. For example, on a curve of any significance your car will stick to the road better under very slight acceleration in 3rd than it will in top with your foot off the accelerator at the same speed. Approaching a bend always slow down a little *more* than is strictly required, especially when vision is restricted. Change down *before* you arrive so that you are geared to resume slight acceleration as you take the bend.

The technique ensures the best balance of the car and reduces the risk of skidding. At a very tight bend, low gear may need to be 2nd rather than 3rd.

The principle of taking turns under slight acceleration rather than trailing throttle (foot off accelerator) applies across the spectrum. Thus, although you may not need to change down for a slight curve, you should still reduce speed in advance so as to take the bend under slight power.

Having talked about how good anticipation, gear selection and timing make braking other than lightly a rarity for the best drivers, we need to examine times when, although they are not emergencies, you have to use your brakes firmly to slow or stop. That is, times when taking your foot off the accelerator and changing down will be insufficient and the footbrake must come in to get speed down.

BRAKES

Braking should be gentle, progressive, sufficient for the task, never overdone. Bad anticipation and then ill-judged excessive braking is one cause of the high percentage of accidents which are rear-end shunts.

Your first "live" encounter with the footbrake in Lesson 3 should have shown the respect it demands if you are to avoid skids and accidents. At higher speeds problems magnify. Carefully measured brake application, matching its severity to room available, becomes increasingly crucial.

Imagine you need to slow quite quickly from 45 mph and perhaps stop. You start braking progressively and change down to 3rd. However, by the time you feel 3rd helping the brakes, circumstances have changed and you realise that a stop will not be needed. You continue braking only as much as the situation demands. You also get down to 2nd both to assist the braking further and to prepare for re-acceleration soon after you are able to release the brakes.

Suppose on the other hand there has been no change and you do need to stop. You need not get down to 2nd; stay in 3rd and stop with the footbrake.

In all your braking, start a fraction earlier than necessary if you can. "Meter" your braking effort evenly across the distance available. At no stage brake harder than necessary.

But make sure you *can* stop – or have speed down comfortably if that's all that's needed – *short* of wherever you must.

Why start early and aim "comfortably short"? Two reasons: (a) You will then have room to ease off just before finally stopping, as taught in Lesson 3. (b) More important, you build in a margin of safety. You confirm your brake power *before* running out of time for dealing with an unexpectedly skiddy surface, having your foot slip off the pedal, brake failure or other mishap. Such horrors happen rarely but you will be glad of good habits when they do.

DRIVING LAW

Imagine that your mother or perhaps your child has just been killed by a reckless driver. How would you feel? It is a terrifying thought that you could drive away from your home and moments later kill or maim an innocent person. You would have to pay – not just the due punishment under the law but worse – you would pay with remorse all your life.

Please forgive the morbid picture but it happens – most days. The law spells out a driver's serious obligations so that no one can be in any doubt:

"YOU MUST NOT DRIVE
- RECKLESSLY.
- WITHOUT DUE CARE AND ATTENTION.
- WITHOUT REASONABLE CONSIDERATION FOR OTHER PERSONS USING THE ROAD".

Almost every important driving rule can be classified under one of these three commands, from recklessness such as excessive speeding or drunken driving, to inattentive failure to pay heed to what other drivers are doing, or perhaps inconsiderate refusal to give way.

In the back of your Highway Code is a section entitled 'The Law's Demands'. You will find the basic obligations above under the sub-sections: 'When Driving You Must' and '(When Driving) You Must Not'. Other legal requirements you need to be aware of are there too. It helps to remember these additional points if you classify each of them in your own mind under one of the three overall headings above. Choosing the category for each rule makes you think harder about it.

PARKING LAW

Not only does the law demand your full attention while driving, it requires that you park safely. Find 'Waiting and Parking' in the main part of your Highway Code. Compare the rules there with the laws which reinforce them under 'When You Stop <u>You Must</u>' and '(When You Stop) <u>You Must Not</u>' at the back. That process should help you learn the rules.

Whenever you are out (not just on lessons) study parking habits. You will discover parking laziness, indifference, and illegality everywhere. Imagine you are a policeman and decide which drivers you would bring to book. Even if you confine yourself to parkers causing danger you will find books-full. See how many obscure offences you can spot too.

Make sure you know the rules on parking lights at night. It may not be dark when you park but you must always consider whether it will be before you return, and also whether you are facing the correct way.

Suppose you see a car parked on a narrow road causing a queue of traffic to form before people can pass. Whoever parked it there is breaking the Highway Code and the Law, and provoking frustration amongst drivers being obstructed. That frustration may lead to an accident though not necessarily at the site of the "crime". The guilty parker must surely accept some blame morally if not legally. Such parking can hardly be viewed as being with "reasonable consideration" either.

The Highway Code uses the terms "waiting" and "let your vehicle stand" as well as "parking". That means you can't ignore rules just because you are sitting in the car!

SIGNS AND SIGNALS

The examiner will expect you to interpret *all* signs and signals correctly. He will probably ask you questions on one or two you don't happen to see during the driven part of your Test. They can all be found towards the back of your Highway Code under:- Light signals controlling traffic; Signals by authorised persons; Signals to other road users; Traffic signs; Road markings.

We will follow the same order here, starting with traffic

lights. To obey traffic lights you must understand their sequence. Driving towards an amber light, what can you expect to come next? You cannot be in the correct gear at the right speed unless you know! Confirm the order with your instructor. Test your own retention of the sequence next time you can stand near a traffic light and watch the phasing. Although the timing of each set of lights is different, notice how long each colour or combination of colours is shown. See also Situation Six later in this lesson, and Lesson 7, page 114.

The meaning of each phase is laid down in the Code. Take care to understand the detail. For example, green will not always mean "go". Have a look.

"Authorised persons" who give signals include not only policemen, but traffic wardens, and school crossing patrols. When signalled to STOP, you MUST. However, when beckoned forward, it is YOUR responsibility to look out for other traffic and pedestrians, just as at a green traffic light.

Signals used to flag your INTENTIONS to other road users include direction indicators and arm signals. Remember you use them to warn; their use doesn't confer any right to go ahead. You first make sure other road users are accepting your signal. Practise the arm signal actions as you look at the Code. (You don't need to be in the car.) Notice the difference between the arm signal for "I intend to move in to the left" and for "I intend to slow down or stop". When you want to pull in and stop on the left you use the first signal above, NOT the second. The most important use for the second signal – and one examiners especially look for – is on the approach to a zebra crossing. When someone is about to cross (or has started) it warns traffic all around that you are pulling up, as well as reassuring the pedestrian.

Traffic signs in the Highway Code are divided into groups, most of the signs in each group having a common shape. This helps remember them. Within each group the signs most frequently met are in the first few rows. Concentrate there to start with. You will need to come back to this part of the Code again and again as you prepare for your Test, to be certain you can correctly interpret every sign.

A good way to learn each page of signs is to cover the main body of the page, leaving the top row of signs on show but not their meanings printed underneath. You can then try to identify all the signs in the row before you check your accuracy. When you think you know the top line reveal the second line, and so on. You need not worry about the pages on Direction Signs just yet but when you have studied all the others you can consolidate your knowledge by working back *up* each page, this time trying to visualise the appropriate sign for each meaning before revealing the correct answer. Signs where the meaning of the symbol is not self-evident, e.g. 'No Entry', 'No Stopping', 'Priority over vehicles from opposite direction', demand feats of memory their designers can surely have never considered! Notice how the angle or direction of a symbol can alter the meaning. For example, without looking, draw yourself a leftwards first double bend sign, then a rightwards first one. Did you get them correct – and inside a triangle the right way up?

Lastly, we come to road markings. The most essential ones you must know before getting out on the road are the white line road markings.

Yellow lines at the edge of the road restrict parking and waiting. All you really need to know about them for the purpose of your Test is the more yellow paint you see, the tougher the restriction. Signs attached to lamp posts etc. always accompany the lines to tell you local rules.

Notice one very fierce zig-zag yellow line however; at a school entrance you may not even stop to let your child in or out of the car. You must park elsewhere and walk along.

A few more white and yellow road markings round off this part of the Code, including layouts for box junctions, zebra crossings and so on. All are important to know. For example, if you are driving in a lane marked with a white arrow – head angled to the left – and you drive straight on, you could be accused of careless driving.

On the road you will sometimes see traffic signs mounted one above the other. The uppermost sign should normally be the one which denotes the first of the hazards you will reach.

TRAFFIC PRIORITIES

A popular and dangerous myth among drivers is that in certain circumstances RIGHT-OF-WAY exists for them.

Rules of the Road may imply greater priority to one party than another but this notion "MY RIGHT-OF-WAY" is false. In an accident, to say that you took no avoiding action because it was your "Right-of-Way" is no justification. Courts award judgments accordingly. However, where one driver in an accident has ignored some Rule of the Road he will usually be held mainly (or wholly) at fault. He will be more likely to receive a stiff penalty and/or be landed with a hefty increase in his motor insurance.

Here are six traffic priority questions. See if you agree with my answers which follow. Whilst considering these situa-

SITUATION ONE – fig. 13

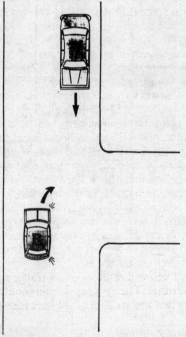

Fig. 13

Car 'A' is going straight ahead. Car 'B' wants to turn right. Who has precedence? Why?

tions to identify the where/when/why of basic Rules of the Road in respect of 'who goes first' will help.

Two principles over-ride everything. The first principle over-rides the second one as well. It is that pedestrians DO have RIGHT-OF-WAY – always. You must never even frighten, never mind harm them. Whose priority it may be is irrelevant. They do not need to use a pedestrian crossing to command precedence. They have it wherever they are by

SITUATION TWO – fig. 14

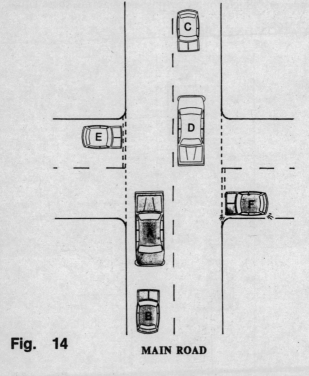

Fig. 14   **MAIN ROAD**

Car 'E' is waiting to cross over a major road. Car 'F' is waiting to turn left into the major road. To which other cars must 'E' give way? To which other cars must 'F' give way? If 'F' were turning right instead, to which other cars would it then have to give way?

virtue of the fact you dare not hit them and risk being charged with manslaughter. I will return to pedestrians later.

The second principle is that no other driver should ever be forced to swerve or slow down because of your driving. Drivers often co-operate by changing speed or steering to accommodate each others' well-signalled manoeuvres. Never rely on such goodwill until certain! It only takes you a single move out of turn to find you have broken this principle by causing someone to have to take avoiding action.

SITUATION THREE – fig. 15

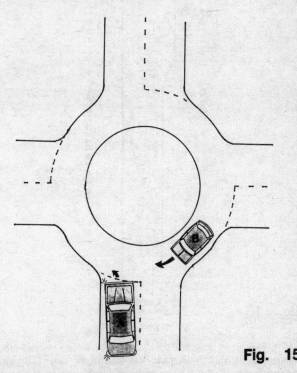

Fig. 15

Car 'A' wants to join the roundabout while 'B' is already on it. Who has priority?

SITUATION FOUR – fig. 16

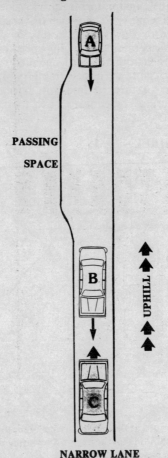

Fig. 16

Car 'B' is going downhill on a steep narrow lane and has met 'C' coming uphill. Car 'A' is some way behind 'B'. Car 'C' ought to have priority. 'B' should reverse back until opposite the passing place. 'A' should wait where he is 'til he sees how things develop. Why?

SITUATION FIVE – fig. 17

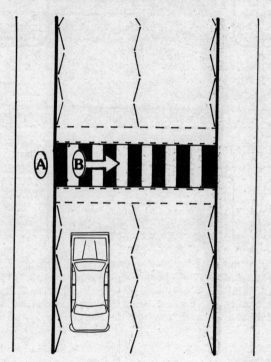

Fig. 17

The car has stopped at the zebra crossing. Pedestrian 'B' is on it. Pedestrian 'A' is standing on the pavement waiting to cross. Which of the pedestrians has Right-of-Way?

SITUATION SIX – fig. 18

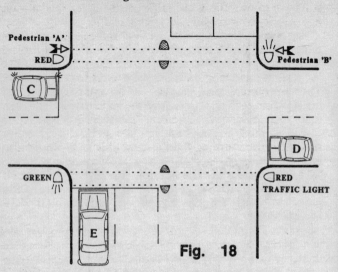

Fig. 18

Car 'E' is about to move on at the green traffic light, while 'C' and 'D' are at red. Car 'C' will be turning left when the lights change. Pedestrians 'A' and 'B' are preparing to cross. When car 'E' travels straight ahead on green whom should the driver look out for? When car 'C' comes to turn left, to whom must he give way?

ANSWER ONE

Car 'A'. In the United Kingdom the fundamental Rule of the Road is we DRIVE ON THE LEFT. Vehicles doing so have a general priority over those wishing to cross their path. Car 'B' must wait in the position shown until 'A' has passed. He would only turn ahead of 'A' if there was plenty of time to do so *without causing* 'A' *to slow down*. The judgment of when to wait and when to go will be gained with experience, and guidance from your instructor.

ANSWER TWO

Car 'E' must give way to all four cars 'A' to 'D'. (Had 'A'

and 'B' not been there and 'D' been further past, 'E' would still have to wait for 'C'.) Traffic on the major road always has priority over crossing or joining traffic.

At every intersection with an important major road, the minor roads have either a thick white 'Stop' line or broken 'Give Way' double lines painted across them. 'Stop' or 'Give Way' signs command the side road drivers to cede priority. The appropriate sign, warning of an intersection, alerts drivers from each direction along the major road so they can reduce speed and take extra care despite having priority.

Car 'F' must give way to cars 'D' and 'C' on the major road. If it were turning right instead of left, 'F' would also have to give way to cars 'A', 'B' and 'E'. It would give way to 'E' because its turn would be across the path of that car. (If you imagine the two side roads joined across as one for a moment you can see that 'E' is simply 'driving on the left' just as 'A' is in Situation One.)

Sometimes on quiet country roads or housing estates you will come across junctions unmarked as to priority. It is then the duty of drivers from ALL directions to take extreme care. Always slow down sufficiently to let others go first. If the intersection is blind, this may entail a stop before you can be sure your way is clear. Courtesy and common sense have to prevail in the absence of any 'clues'. Your speed must be down to a crawl so you can stop instantly if necessary. Never assume what another driver will do; watch what he *is* doing. Where your unmarked road, meeting another one, forms a T, drivers on that road will expect to go first. You would be bound to be crossing or joining their path. However, when an unmarked junction is forked like a Y it can be impossible to define which road joins the other. The best advice then is to let others go first. If there is any question you may be crossing someone's path, wait. Be especially wary when it appears you are merely going straight on on your leg of the fork. That may mirror exactly what a driver on the other leg thinks he is doing!

ANSWER THREE

Car 'B'. On roundabouts, the rule is you give way to traffic from your right. That means traffic already on a roundabout has priority over joining traffic. There are a few exceptions to meet the needs of local traffic flows. Where they occur, white 'Give Way' road markings combined with 'Give Way' signposts clearly denote the reversed priorities.

ANSWER FOUR

Car 'C' has priority because it is travelling uphill. That is the general rule on narrow roads and places where width may be restricted temporarily. The rule must be interpreted with commonsense. If car 'B' was hauling a heavy caravan, it would be silly to insist that it should reverse. Instead, car 'C' should reverse back to a point where the two can pass, thus showing "reasonable consideration for other persons using the road". On the other hand, if driver 'A' was also towing a wide load and car 'C' had already set off forwards again, it would be reasonable to expect 'A' to wait opposite the passing place until 'C' could squeeze into it. Consult your Highway Code about single track roads. There is more to know.

ANSWER FIVE

Most people will quickly and correctly agree that pedestrian 'B' has Right-of-Way because he is on the crossing. But what about pedestrian 'A' who hasn't yet stepped on to the crossing itself? Has he no rights?

Pedestrian 'A' also enjoys potential Right-of-Way *because he is there* close to the pavement edge. Pedestrians are more easily damaged than cars! (In this respect the proximity of the zebra crossing is unimportant. No legal system could countenance wilful slaughter just because individuals stray on to roads other than at crossings.) No one denies that pedestrians *should* take care and nothing written here loses sight of that. But the law must and does put the onus on drivers to take all possible avoiding action when a pedestrian steps out whatsoever the circumstances.

Although the precise zebra crossing rule is that drivers need only stop if someone has a foot on the crossing, we can now look again at 'A'. As 'A' is standing so close, there has to be a reasonable assumption that he intends to step on to the crossing. All drivers approaching from either direction must be prepared to stop. That means slowing down sufficiently to be able to stop quickly if he moves. Imagine yourself at the wheel arriving at the scene. First you slow right down. Then you observe 'A' carefully. You judge from his stance whether he has seen you and is waiting for you to pass (after pedestrian 'B' clears), or whether he is going to step on to the crossing. If he is clearly waiting, you go carefully on, making sure 'B' is well over half way across beforehand so that you cannot possibly alarm him. If 'A' does step out, you stop. If you are in any doubt, you stop. (You can always go on if it then becomes clear he is not wanting to cross yet.) At crossings it is best to stop a bonnet's length back from the painted line. This allows pedestrians to watch behind you more easily, in case someone attempts to shoot past illegally. People cross more quickly if they feel unharassed too.

Pedestrians then, *regardless of crossings*, ALL command your "due care and attention". Don't forget they may be deaf, blind, juvenile, drunk, chasing a wounded animal – anything. Protect them all.

ANSWER SIX

Drivers are duty-bound to avoid accidents. Driver 'E' must ensure that both cars 'C' and 'D' have or remain stopped. He must also look out for other vehicles such as motorcyclists who may suddenly appear from behind 'C' or 'D' in a cloud of vrrooom!!! He must be prepared to stop for pedestrians 'A' or 'B' should either step out.

When car 'C' turns left he must be prepared to wait for both pedestrians to cross. As noted in Answer Five, pedestrians rule anyway but here they also have the green light in *their* favour and, if you think about it, 'C' is turning across their path. 'C' must also have a wary eye that 'D' doesn't suddenly decide to turn right and break all rules by trying to cut across in front.

PASSING PARKED VEHICLES

Imagine that you are driving along with other traffic coming towards you on the opposite side of the road. You see a car parked ahead *on your side*. You note that there is insufficient room on your side for you to pass it. The Rule of the Road is that you must slow down and/or stop before reaching the parked car, giving way to the oncoming traffic. You must wait until there is a sufficient gap or clearance on the opposite side, for you to pass the parked car without anyone coming needing to slow down. The correct position to wait is shown by car 'B' in fig. 2, page 25. (Often a wide-awake and courteous approaching driver, who sees room to do so, will move in to his left a little to make room for you to go earlier than would otherwise be possible.)

Parking in many residential streets narrows them in effect to single track roads. Where this happens treat them as such, as for Situation Four just now. If there are no gaps in the parking to wait in or opposite, you may need to pause to let someone out before fully entering the street. Tuck in as much as you can because main road traffic from behind you won't see why you are having to wait.

PRIVATE DRIVEWAYS AND PAVEMENTS

When you enter or leave a narrow entrance or gateway you cannot just shoot in or out. You must first give way to anyone walking along the pavement. It is *their* path you will be crossing. If there are tall hedges or fences you dare not do more than nose forward out of a gateway until you can see it's safe. Equally, if you are turning in to a driveway, pedestrians must be free to go first. As the Highway Code says "pavements are for people – not motor vehicles".

In your Highway Code is a section devoted to 'The Safety of Pedestrians' where you will find a great deal more a driver must know. While you study it, compare zebra and pelican crossings so that you know exactly how each must be treated.

LANE DISCIPLINE

In the Highway Code, under the headings 'Lines and Lanes Along the Road' and 'Overtaking' are a group of vital rules you must know. Read through them first if you haven't already. Refer to the back of the Code under 'Road Markings' for illustrations of the different types of line.

One principle of lanes you must put first: where you have a choice of lanes you must NEVER change without using your mirrors then a signal – NEVER be the cause of anyone having to swerve or slow down. Woolly or absent lane change signalling is a common accident cause. Anyone who overtakes you (or passes on your left in a queue or one-way street) should reasonably be able to expect that you will stick to your lane.

A second principle of lanes for all roads other than one-way streets is that, out of two or more lanes in your direction, you should drive in the left hand one unless you are passing a parked vehicle, overtaking or turning right. Having used an outer lane (other than for turning) you should return to the leftmost lane at the earliest possible moment. This is a fundamental addition to the rule met in Situation One a few pages ago that we DRIVE ON THE LEFT.

The rule does NOT extend to passing on the left. That is only allowed at well-defined places you must learn from the 'Overtaking' section of your Highway Code. Everywhere else, if a driver ahead is using an outer lane, he is entitled to feel safe to move in without hindrance.

Creeping up and then "hanging" close to his inside tail is bad driving. It puts doubt in his mind about your intentions and stops him moving over. If others cannot then pass him you contribute to the moving obstruction offence dealt with shortly. When you are catching up someone in an outside lane who doesn't seem to be going to turn right, you should move out behind him (remember principle one of lanes just above!) and follow at a sensible distance 'til he moves in. Hoot or flash your headlights after a while if you think he doesn't know you are there, which may prompt him to move.

A third principle connected with lanes also concerns a driver feeling safe to move in, as above, in this case after overtaking. Because you are driving along in a lane does not mean you own it! Imagine here that you are being passed on a road with only one lane in each direction. The overtaker is therefore using the opposing carriageway. You must be prepared to slow down to make a safe gap for him to move in to. An unexpected change in the overtaking picture may mean he has to "dive" in fast at any stage. Watch and hold his gap until you see no more is needed. Do not be tempted to speed up when someone passes you. You could become part cause of a head-on smash.

MOVING OBSTRUCTION

Drivers have been fined for causing a moving obstruction. We drive in the lefthandmost lane so that a right hand lane or lanes are kept free for overtaking or turning right. If you block an outer lane when you are neither overtaking nor turning, and prevent others from passing, you are causing an obstruction, even though you may be going at the speed limit. Others reasonably expect you to move over. It is not for you to "decide" how fast they may go. The moving obstructor causes immense frustration and anger which leads to nose-to-tail driving and accidents. On roads such as fast-flowing suburban through routes, an unnecessarily full outer lane also prevents anyone who is turning right from being noticed far enough in advance. If he has to stop before he can make his turn, instead of a very few drivers behind him seeing that they will need to filter inwards to pass on his left, a dangerous bottleneck suddenly strikes the outside lane. Everyone in it has to stop sharply. They become an instant queue. Drivers in the left lane correctly pass on by. Until they have gone or the driver turning right clears, none of the stopped drivers can move.

TURNING OBSTRUCTION

Suppose you mistakenly enter a lane with a green filter arrow reserved for a left or right hand turn. When the green arrow lights up you must take that turn. You must not obstruct correctly-positioned left-turners behind you.

If you haven't already been able to do so, discuss this lesson together with your instructor. He can then give you the short quiz which follows.

HAND BOOK BACK TO INSTRUCTOR

ASSESSMENT

It is intended for you to run through this home-study lesson and ask your learner questions on it so that you can assess and devote extra time to anything he finds hard. Below is a quiz to give on Highway Code topics the lesson suggested he should look at.

HIGHWAY CODEBREAKER

1. Q. What may you *not* do with rear fog-lamps?
    A. Dazzle others. They must only be on when visibility is *seriously* reduced, defined as being under 100 metres.

2. Q. Can you park where there is a double white line if the broken line is on your side?
    A. No.

3. Q. If a street is no more than $3\frac{1}{2}$ cars wide and there is a car parked on the opposite side where you intend to pull in, what should you do?
    A. You must either park further on or join him on the other side if safe. To stop opposite him would leave less than two vehicle widths between you, a dangerous narrowing of the road.

4. Q. Name the one circumstance at the wheel in darkness when your headlamps must be switched off.
    A. When you are pulled in at the kerbside, e.g. to check a map or whatever. Shining headlamps on a stationary vehicle create a "staring" dazzle for others.

5. Q. In a traffic hold-up what is meant by "jumping the queue" which the Code directs you must not do?
    A. Cutting in to an adjacent lane, or overtaking those already waiting. Barging in and out unprepared to take your turn is inconsiderate driving. When a queue develops, an intelligent choice of lane if there is one may save you time. But it should be taken well before you might be accused of queue-hopping, and then stuck to.

6. Q. Which Highway Code advice about overtaking over-rides the rest?
    A. IF IN DOUBT – DO NOT OVERTAKE.

7.   Q. Name three major obligations upon drivers, each
         starting with "You must not drive . . .
     A. . . . recklessly"; . . . without due care and atten-
         tion"; . . . without reasonable consideration for
         other persons using the road".

8.   Q. Where must you not allow your vehicle to stand?
     A. There are many answers. Check them all in your
         Highway Code under 'Waiting and Parking', and in
         the Law's Demands under 'When you stop – you
         <u>must not</u>".

9.   Q. What must you *not* do when approaching a zebra
         crossing?
     A. You must NOT within the zig-zag lined area (or its
         equivalent if unmarked) overtake the moving vehicle
         nearest the crossing, or the leading vehicle which
         has stopped. Nor, for the sake of a space or two
         moved up in a traffic queue, may you sit on the
         crossing blocking the way of people walking across,
         whether or not you happen to be there first. You
         may neither park nor wait anywhere inside the zig-
         zag area.

10. Q. What is the normal sequence of traffic light signals?
         How do pelican crossing lights differ?
     A. Red. Red and amber. Green. Amber. Red. At
         pelican lights a flashing amber signal on its own is
         substituted for red and amber. During the flashing
         amber phase you wait for any pedestrians still about
         but you can (and do) go on if it is clear. You don't
         have to wait for green. However, notice that a slow
         pedestrian may equally mean that on green you still
         can't go immediately.

11. Ask your pupil to demonstrate each of the 'Signals by
     authorised persons' as found in the Highway Code and
     then to do the same for the arm signals drivers use.

12. Test your learner on a variety of traffic signs (ignore
     direction signs) and road markings. A quick way is to

cover up the meaning of the item where it appears in the Code while you show him the symbol or picture.

13. Q. When do pedestrians have Right-of-Way over cars?
    A. ALWAYS.(See pages 80 and 86.)

14. Q. You stop for a pedestrian to cross. How soon do you move on: a) at a traffic light or police controlled crossing? b) at a pelican crossing? c) at a zebra crossing? d) wherever the person may have chosen to cross – being elsewhere than on a crossing?
    A. For a) and b) directly the lights change in your favour or the policeman or traffic warden beckons you forward *provided* that all the pedestrians who set off from either kerb have passed well clear of you. Never trust the lights or the traffic controller. Watch the pedestrians yourself. They often ignore rules anyway. For c) and d) simply wait 'til all the pedestrians in both directions are safely across well past you. Never rev your engine, creep forward or 'hurry' them. Never move so soon after someone passes as to frighten but, unless lights or the person in authority still hold you, you need not wait 'til they reach their opposite kerb.

It is worth making out the usual assessment checklist to give your learner so that he can judge his success against the objectives of this lesson. Use your Progress Chart to mark gaps in his knowledge needing to be filled later. There may be some that are essential to sort out before he can drive round the quiet route suggested in the next lesson. Agree times to test any missing knowledge and for Lesson 5. Should you both feel that a repeat session on this lesson will be helpful beforehand, give the book back to your trainee for the time being.

LESSON 5

STEERING AND GEAR CHANGING

OBJECTIVES

For your learner to be able to:-
1. Pull away from behind a parked vehicle.
2. Change smoothly up and down through the gears.
3. Drive a short, quiet route taking in left and right turns.
4. Stop adjacent to a pre-selected marker-point: (a) normally, (b) quickly.

IMPORTANT NOTE

When your learner is driving, keep reminding yourself he has not got your experience and judgment in reading the road. All he has is his own fledgling judgment. He will be slow to relate what he sees to what he must do. He often won't react as quickly to a worsening traffic situation as you expect unless you put in a well-timed cue-word. So avoid last-minute instructions or warnings. They can be dangerous.

Whilst letting him do the driving and make his mistakes where they don't matter, you must regard yourself as the back-up eyes and brains. In all the lessons which follow, the same applies, especially when something new and/or unexpected arises. Note that he may not get something right a second time or even a third. You cannot relax just because you have pointed out a mistake once! So do watch out!

LOCATION and DURATION

Choose a quiet time and location. You must drive there. The ideal is a short circuit without hills, covering left and right turns (mostly left hand) and leading back to where you started. A reasonably long straight is needed at the beginning to allow your learner to practise Stages 1–5 without having to turn. You will need an hour to an hour and a half. Do take one or two little breaks because you can guarantee this will be more tiring than most learners like to admit.

BRIEFING

Promise your learner that as in Lesson 3 you will demonstrate or explain each objective before he has a go. Reassure him that when he first drives the circuit you will instruct him exactly how to cope with each junction and with other vehicles. This is the time to say that you will frequently be asking him to pull in to the side of the road, perhaps to brief him on a tricky situation ahead, maybe to discuss something that has just happened. If your Progress Chart is signalling unfinished business from Lesson 4 or earlier, it's best to deal with it before the lesson starts. Such matters slide all too easily.

LESSON PLAN

STAGE 1 – Demonstrate how to move away from behind a pretend parked vehicle. Denote a tree or lamp post etc. near to the start of your long straight, to indicate the parked vehicle. (Your learner can try with a real car later – in Stage 6.) Spell out each factor – especially as regards other traffic – as you demonstrate, so your learner can see the extra steering, clutch slipping and visual skill needed when a parked vehicle complicates moving off. It is a manoeuvre he can expect to meet on Test.

STAGE 2 – Demonstrate changing up through the gears from 1st to 4th. Comment on the road SPEED at which you make the changes and ensure that your learner listens to the SOUND of the engine each time. Do not exceed 30 mph. Your learner needs to see that getting up the gearbox smartly doesn't require much speed. You don't want a pupil who never gets above 3rd in a 30 mph speed limit!

STAGE 3 – As you are going along, mention how often you use your mirrors and comment on any other traffic about. Demonstrate changing back down to 2nd in order to slow down. Again point out SPEED and SOUND. From 2nd go back up to top.

STAGE 4 – Next, mentioning your specific mirrors' check first, show how to bring the car gently to a stop on the footbrake, getting down to 3rd as you do so but without troubling to take 2nd. Remind your learner how, in circumstances where you know you are going to stop, there is no need to use 2nd.

STAGE 5 – With no delay, in case traffic appears behind (as emphasised in Lesson 3), move on and then repeat Stages 2 to 4. As before, explain what you are doing in respect of other traffic that may come into view ahead or behind. This time in Stage 4 add left indicator to your specific mirrors' check, and finish by showing him how to pull in to the kerbside correctly.

Unless there is still enough straight road in front for your learner comfortably to complete all these five stages, turn the car round, then switch off the engine and change over seats.

STAGE 6 – Encourage any questions before your pupil starts to practise Stages 1 to 5. Ask him to keep you informed of decisions he is making from the moment he starts driving. This helps you correct errors straightaway. Let him repeat these five stages several times, with you turning the car round for him after Stage 5 each time if necessary. For the first few times a pretend car is best for Stage 1.

Watch carefully. Only prompt if necessary. Check he omits nothing from the "cockpit" drill, start-up routine or move-off procedure. He MUST turn his head and look behind at the correct moment before moving off. On the move, get him using the mirrors frequently, as well as specifically before slowing down. Correct order and routine on the controls when he stops must be followed: handbrake on, gear to neutral, before feet come off the pedals.

When he pulls in at the kerbside, check that he is no more than 6"–9" (15cm–23cm) out. If not, or if his tyres have struck the kerb, make him get out of the car and look for himself (be sure he checks behind before opening the door!).

That's the best way for him to learn to connect what he sees from the driving seat with the true position of the wheels. Getting out to look can do with plenty of repetition 'til practice makes perfect. Make sure the kerbside is always approached gently enough to avoid tyre damage should he hit it.

If he is doing well in all the Stages then find a parked vehicle for him to practise Stage 1 once or twice 'for real' before you stop the practice. If none is handy you can always do it later. A break to discuss progress is probably a good idea before Stage 7.

STAGE 7 – You demonstrate the third objective by driving round your chosen route. At all times keep your learner informed about where your eyes are searching in case other traffic appears. That apart, concentrate your commentary at each turn on one aspect of how you tackle it. This enables you to introduce the complete drill, point by point. Although I describe everything in five examples, you will need a few extra turnings in order to apply the teaching to a variety of turns, both right and left.

– **First Turn:** (Make this a turn off whatever road you are on.) Ask your pupil to watch your distance from the kerb or your place beside the centre line on the approach, and then exactly how you handle the STEERING WHEEL into the turn and for straightening up.

– **Second Turn:** Introduce the Highway Code maxim – MIRRORS – SIGNAL – MANOEUVRE. Point out by when your preparatory mirrors' checks should be complete and the moment to start your indicator signal.

– **Third Turn:** (Arrange to be emerging to join another road.) Describe how you scan your eyes around the whole area on the approach, how you look out for anyone on foot about to cross the end of your road as you reach it, and so on. At the junction itself, instil the routine "LOOK RIGHT, LEFT AND RIGHT AGAIN". Show how you make it an integral part of your scanning. Emphasise how, if you have to stop and wait, you then repeat the routine possibly many times until there is a safe gap in the traffic and that you always include a final look R, L and R just prior to moving.

– **Fourth Turn:** In a repeat of emerging to join another

road, concentrate on your POSITIONING. Discuss your distance out from the kerb in relation to which way you are turning. Show your pupil how you stop with your front bumper at the line (visualizing one if there is no line painted) neither – like many learners – half a car's length before it, which prevents looking R, L and R again properly, nor over it which could be dangerous.

– **Fifth Turn:** Talk about TIMING. Include when to take your foot off the accelerator on approach before changing down, and so on. On turns that don't involve a stop, ask him to watch carefully so he knows what the minimum speed you get down to feels like. Most beginners try to turn too fast, swinging out as a result and frightening themselves if not others.

Continue to drive round your circuit now marrying the elements together for each type of turn: steering action; Mirrors– Signal– Manoeuvre; LOOK RIGHT, LEFT AND RIGHT AGAIN; positioning; timing.

STAGE 8 – Drive round your circuit having your learner *talk you through* every action. This should reveal any misunderstandings before he takes over.

STAGE 9 – Before your learner attempts the circuit explain that to begin with you want him to pull in safely after each turn. Give him your reason, which is to allow you to examine together and undistracted, his conduct of individual turns while good and not-so-good points remain fresh.

For yourself, remember your reassurance to him about exact instructions during the first circuit! For example, when other traffic enters the picture, stipulate what to do at once before he starts to worry. By the time he is on to a second time around you should be able to dispense with pulling in except for turns which are still producing any major error.

Be prepared to be shocked by your pupil's initial ineptitude! Unless he's amazingly proficient on this first drive you are going to find, amongst other problems:

- failure to tuck quickly enough into a turn and/or to straighten up after it.
- letting go of steering wheel in mid-turn, especially if a kerb has been mounted. Holding or using it incorrectly.

- looking down at controls instead of ahead.
- forgetting to look ahead down a road being turned in to (very common).
- not noticing other people on the road *even though you may have seen him look their way*.
- forgetting clutch principles in excitement.
- stalling. Then forgetting what he has been taught to do to recover.

Remember after you start him off that if a problem, like misjudgment of distance from the kerb when pulling in, is going to recede with practice, you need not make much of it although you must never let it become a habit. But a fundamental snag like wandering across to the wrong side of the road must be resolved at once. Discussion at the road side should elicit why it is happening so that cure can be direct and permanent.

Assuming good progress, go on to Stage 10. I recommend a few minutes' break first unless you're certain neither of you needs it!

STAGE 10 – There should be no need to demonstrate the fourth objective. Select a prominent post or marker at the roadside well away from junctions or obstructions. Ask your learner to drive towards the marker at about 10–15 mph and stop normally (evenly with light braking) alongside it. Select different markers and repeat this once or twice. When he is able successfully to judge a stop from that speed, increase the initial pace to 20 mph for some further repeats.

Once competent from the higher speed revert to 10–15 mph and ask for a quicker, evenly-braked stop. Explain that this is NOT a full Emergency Stop but the development of distance judgment for the Quick-Reaction Stop. Particularly from the higher speed, your learner will see how difficult it can be to stop accurately, safely.

Your learner may be eager to get in more driving time but you should drive home. There is much to be sure he knows before allowing any chance of meeting a situation for which he is not ready.

ASSESSMENT
This might wait until you get home and both have time to

relax. As in earlier lessons, hand your learner an achievement
checklist styled on fig. 10. It can make a useful starting point
for a discussion of the events of the lesson, in which you can
offer praise wherever due and encouragement towards
overcoming problems. If you feel it is necessary, agree a time
for additional practice of any part of this lesson before going
on to Lesson 6. Record whatever you need on your Progress
Chart. To end this lesson, a Highway Code quiz follows.

HIGHWAY CODEBREAKER

1. Q. What does the Code say about other road users in
   connection with your moving off?
   A. "...move off only when you can do so safely
   without making...(them)...change speed or
   direction."

2. Q. What attitude should you adopt to someone
   overtaking you?
   A. Allow him to if he wants. Slow down if necessary.

3. Q. If continuous driving is making you sleepy what
   should you do?
   A. Refresh the air supply inside the car. Stop and rest
   if necessary.

4. Q. When can you cross a double white line solid on
   your side?
   A. To access or leave premises or a side road; when
   ordered to by a policeman or traffic warden; to
   avoid an obstruction.

5. Q. Driving along a single-carriageway road with three
   lanes, when can you use the right hand lane?
   A. Never.

6. Q. When are cyclists less likely to ride straight?
   A. In high winds, and on bad road surfaces.

LESSON 6

COPING WITH HILLS

OBJECTIVES
 For your learner to be able to:-
1. Combine gears, brakes and accelerator to best effect uphill and downhill.
2. Achieve a perfect uphill start no matter how steep.

LOCATION and DURATION
 This lesson is divided into home study and practice and will take about an hour and a half altogether, most of it driving. The practice needs a quiet hilly area.

BRIEFING
 Ask your learner to look through the short home study section before you set off. You could deal with any outstanding matters on your Progress Chart before he begins.

RETURN BOOK TO LEARNER FOR HOME STUDY

UPHILL AND DOWNHILL
 Consider these differences:-

UPHILL
1. More acceleration is needed to maintain speed.
2. Lower gear may be needed for extra power.
3. Even "flat-out" in low gear your speed will drop if the hill is very steep.

4. Less braking is needed for slowing down because the hill assists.

DOWNHILL
1. Less acceleration is needed.
2. Lower gear to introduce engine braking may be necessary to increase control.
3. Additional braking may nevertheless be needed to prevent the car 'running away'.
4. Braking is essential *before* changing down if speed is above the maximum for the next gear down.
5. Greater distance and harder braking are required for stopping because the braking effort is counteracted by the hill.
6. Zero acceleration is needed for moving off on a super-steep downhill in case immediate engine braking is required rather than forward momentum. It may be so steep that only partial brake release can be risked until the slope lessens.

Next refresh your memory of 'Other Gear Changing Principles' related to hills in Lesson 4, page 72. Steep hill warning signs were mentioned there. You can find the symbols under WARNING SIGNS in your Highway Code. The gradient is shown as a percentage, e.g. 10% or 20%. A 10% hill means one unit change in height for each ten units of horizontal distance, as shown by fig. 19. A 20% hill means one unit change in five. For the non-mathematical, the greater the percentage is, the steeper the hill!

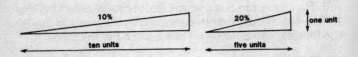

Fig.   19

THE 'HILL START'

Your driving examiner will make sure that you have to move off on a steep uphill at least once during your Test. To move away uphill the routine is identical to that on the level except you use about twice as much accelerator instead of the normal fast idle – but nothing like enough to make the engine scream! The car must not slip backwards. Provided you hold steady that *extra* accelerator, the car will remain still when you release the handbrake. You scotch any forward creep or rolling back by fractionally adjusting the CLUTCH – exactly as you learned in Lesson 3, Stage 2, page 56. When ready to move away you simply combine further modest acceleration with the normal MOVE AWAY steps also found in Lesson 3, Stage 2.

As a beginner, I once found myself on a steep incline at a red traffic light. A Rolls Royce stopped close behind. The thought of the cost of his hand-made radiator grille, not to mention his paintwork, was a marvellous incentive to a good hill start and one you may like to visualise to your own benefit!

GETTING INTO 1ST GEAR ON THE MOVE

You need this occasional manoeuvre at times such as when you turn off a level road into a very steep uphill, or you find a crawling traffic jam ahead on a sharp uphill. It is easy provided your speed in 2nd is down to just above stalling point. Trying to make the change earlier will only crunch the gears.

Make the change deftly so that your left foot can be back up off the clutch and your right foot re-accelerating briskly before your forward momentum can turn into a backward roll! If you are too late and the car begins to hover before rolling backwards, simply pop the clutch down and apply the footbrake to hold you. Then make a full hill start.

HAND BOOK BACK TO INSTRUCTOR

You are ready for the uphill task!

LESSON PLAN

STAGE 1 – Until Lesson 8, your learner is not ready to drive straight from home or back there afterwards. He needs the home study of Lesson 7. His handling of the car, as taught in this lesson, needs to have reached a good standard. Plunging into traffic too early will only wreck his confidence. Before handing over when you arrive at your chosen hilly territory, demonstrate as many of the items on the list of differences your pupil has studied on page 101 as you can. Be sure to include a couple each of uphill and downhill starts and of changing into 1st on the move. For the second time round on each item let your pupil take over the commentary. If he says the wrong thing, do it if it's safe. That will impress the error beautifully!

STAGE 2 – When he's ready to take the wheel remind him that all safety drills will be his responsibility; you will merely give route directions and ask for demonstrations of techniques at appropriate places. Remind yourself to be ever-ready to warn or instruct in good time. There will be plenty of new mistakes – and old ones revisited!

STAGE 3 – Set him off. Observe his co-ordination of gears, accelerator and brakes driving uphill and downhill. Only intervene if he makes a serious mistake, if he asks for advice, or if he starts to go too fast or too slow through poor technique.

STAGE 4 – Tell him to pull in on a downhill; then move away when ready. Watch him on safety as well as correct technique.

STAGE 5 – Ask him to pull in near the bottom of a modest upward slope and move away when safe. If he gets it right let him continue. If he makes a hash of it stop him a stone's throw on and repeat the exercise.

STAGE 6 – As for Stage 5 on a steep uphill, the steeper the better.

STAGE 7 – Earlier in this lesson your learner was reminded how – without altering the accelerator position one jot – it is possible to hold the car still, with the clutch at the biting point and after releasing the handbrake. Ask him to demonstrate this now on your steepest uphill. Holding steady for 10–15 seconds should be enough to prove competence without damaging the clutch. As well as holding still, let him (deliberately) show you how to catch rolling back and how to stop creeping forward.

STAGE 8 – The same steep uphill can be used to practise dropping into 1st gear on the move. Suggest he imagines having caught up a long slow convoy and that it is imperative to match their very slow pace.

ASSESSMENT

Hopefully your usual checklist as in fig. 10, page 43, will carry an excellent report of this lesson with few specific lapses to discuss and plenty justifying a "very good" salutation. Write up your Progress Chart. Agree a date for you to review Lesson 7 together; apart from the joint review suggested, it is one for home study for your learner. This lesson can round off with the brief Highway Code-based quiz below.

HIGHWAY CODEBREAKER

1. Q. What extra precautions would you take when parking on a hill?
    A. Leave your car in 1st or reverse gear. (Were the handbrake to fail, the transmission is thus locked in with the engine. The weight of the car, trying to run away down the slope should not be enough to turn an engine held in low gear.) Also turn the steering so that the kerbside front wheel is chocked against the kerb.

2. Q. On hills, what happens to the stopping distances quoted in the Highway Code?
    A. Depending on steepness they shorten comfortably uphill but they lengthen *dramatically* downhill.

3.   Q. Give two examples where safe overtaking or parking
         can be adversely affected by being on a hill.
      A. 1. At or near the brow of a hill.
         2. On a hump backed bridge.

4.   Q. What sorts of signs might you expect among
         mountains?
      A. Double bend; sharp deviation chevrons; steep hill;
         wild, or accompanied, animals; falling rocks; distance
         to tunnel, etc.

5.   Q. A lorry has caught up behind you on a country
         road. Although there is no one in front of you, it
         has no chance of overtaking because of streaming
         oncoming traffic. You are driving quietly and in no
         hurry. A long uphill stretch is ahead. What would
         you do?
      A. Speed up or at least maintain your speed up the hill
         if safe. Lorries lose speed rapidly going uphill, speed
         which they cannot regain until the next downhill.
         By your showing consideration for that lorry up the
         hill, not only will he benefit, the queue which will
         almost certainly be formed behind him, will too.

LESSON 7

A DEEPER LOOK AT HIGHWAY CODE RULES

Home study followed by review and quiz with instructor

OBJECTIVE
For your learner to be able to describe the essential
Highway Code rules about: ★ Driving Along ★ Lines and

Lanes ★ Junctions ★ Turns ★ Roundabouts ★ One-Way Systems ★ Speed Limits.

LOCATION and DURATION
An hour or so of home study, plus review and quiz time.

BRIEFING
Consult your Progress Chart and give your pupil a list (if necessary!) of Highway Code matters he has misunderstood and/or needs to revise along with his study.

RETURN BOOK TO LEARNER

'DRIVING ALONG'
In your Highway Code under the 'Road User on Wheels' you will find the above heading. Please read all the rules there. Three of them merit deeper analysis:-

'USE YOUR MIRRORS OFTEN' – When driving you MUST look where you are going. You can NEVER look at the scenery. At the same time you must discipline your eyes to divert frequently – a split-second at a time – to your mirrors, and occasionally (rapidly) to your speedometer. (See fig. 20.)

A cursory glance in your mirrors just before you change lane or carry out any other manoeuvre is not enough.

You need a continuous review of what is happening behind. Despite your three mirrors being set for the widest combination rear view as in Lesson 2, two wheelers, cars, even lorries, will tail you hidden in your mirrors' blind spots over great distances. Others catching you up very rapidly can slip into a blind spot just at the moment of a mere casual glance in a particular mirror.

The only sure way of knowing who is there at a given second is through habitual regular scanning of your mirrors to pick them up before they may go into hiding. Having said that, you dare not glue your eyes to the mirrors. Glances are best taken when the road ahead is safe. They can be planned into your technique accordingly.

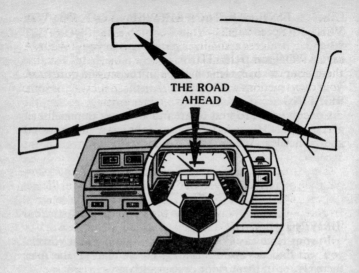

THE ROAD
AHEAD

Fig.   20

Rapid decisions often depend for their safety on up-to-the-second prior knowledge of what's going on behind:

- Whether to try and stop if a green traffic light suddenly changes to amber.
- How much (if at all) you can move out if a parked car door is thrown open in your path.
- When a driver in front makes a late signal for turning right, whether it's safe to filter to his left straightaway. Etc., etc.

One day, a life-saving snap decision may hinge on your mirrors-discipline.

'MIRRORS – SIGNAL – MANOEUVRE' – You need to extend this routine, practised in Lesson 5, to become automatic whenever you: change lanes; slow down; stop; move away; turn; or overtake. Make the mirrors-check specifically the first step every time. Make it in addition to your continuous review I have just described.

'LEAVE ENOUGH SPACE BETWEEN YOU AND THE VEHICLE IN FRONT' – Your Code tables the SHORTEST stopping distances assuming everything is in your favour. A separate diagram, referred to beside the table, helps visualise these distances in car lengths. You will be sensible to assume your own reactions will be slower than those shown, for some time to come. If you're good at memorising, go for the distances for 30, 50 and 70 mph as key ones to remember. But scrutinise the whole table to appreciate just how the distances increase out of all proportion faster than the speeds.

These theoretical distances are no use unless you know what they look like to you. Go out and measure out 75 feet (23 metres), 175 feet (53 metres), and 315 feet (96 metres) from a parked car. Absorb how the distances relate to your eye and then find ANOTHER parked car. This time work by eye first, then measure – and discover how accurate you are.

The distances you now have in your mind's eye have to be increased a dramatic three or fourfold on wet roads.

On snow or ice, stopping distances extend way, way beyond these sorts of measures, even though your maximum speed should never exceed 25–30 mph anyway.

'LINES AND LANES'

A few pages on in your Highway Code comes a section we referred to earlier, in Lesson 4 – 'Lines and Lanes Along the Road'. We next consider less obvious ways in which some of these rules affect you.

The dashes and gaps of a centre line dividing the two halves of an ordinary two-way road are of equal length except where hazards are found. There the dashes are extended and the gaps are reduced to warn you. The danger may be of a hidden dip in the road, of a stretch where vision is restricted, or some other hazardous feature which may not always be thought to merit a separate traffic sign. You see this use of the centre line more in the country than the town. You must learn to 'read' a centre line well ahead so you can slow for each warning and reassess prudent speed. Where the dashes are extended you must not even consider crossing the centre line to overtake unless you can see the road is clear and safe.

Nowadays there are few two-way roads constructed with three lanes. The fatal accident rate for them is too high. Unfortunately, quite a lot of roads divided by a centre line into two lanes are so wide they are treated by everyone as if they have three lanes.

The Code allows you to use a proper middle lane for overtaking or turning right. I suggest that turning right from such a lane (even a genuine one) is too dangerous for any driver, never mind a learner, unless the entire road is empty. Drivers habitually go fast on these roads. They overtake blindly "in convoy" along the middle lane hoping the fellow ahead sees more than they can themselves. If that fellow happens to be you it doesn't seem to enter their heads that you might be signalling, not for overtaking, but to TURN off – let alone that you are slowing down and may need to STOP in that middle lane!

It follows that if you are doing the overtaking you must be ever alert for a right-turner way ahead of you. Notice that, as well as the 'fellow ahead' it could be an oncoming driver whom you were expecting to move in to his own side well before problems arose, that you suddenly appreciate is stopping in the middle. The scene is one in which a multiple shunt can occur in seconds. Make sure you are never a front overtaker caught unawares, or with inexcusable recklessness, a "convoy" idiot too close behind.

Areas of white hatchmarks on the road segregate traffic and protect drivers turning right. If the border is a continuous white line the whole area is a "fattened" double white line which you cannot drive on or over. If the edge is a broken white line the directive is slightly less severe. You can drive over the hatchings but a policeman would expect you to have a very good reason! For example, if you are turning right, moving across ready to take up your turning position earlier than the hatchmarks suggest may be safe and at the same time help followers filter through to your left. In contrast, overtaking through the hatchings, negating their safety function, would be reckless.

"On a three-lane dual carriageway you may stay in the middle lane when there are slower vehicles in the left hand lane". Common misunderstanding of this rule leads to a great deal of obstructive driving. The rule combines with the overtaking rule which commands ". . . move *quickly* past the vehicle you are overtaking . . . then move back to the left side of the road as soon as you can . . .". Failing to regard the two rules in unison and misinterpretation of the first one, which is badly worded, means that many drivers hog a middle lane with an "I have the right to be here" mentality. Absurd and fatal bunching of traffic on our trunk routes and motorways is a direct result. The middle and outside lanes choke up mile after mile and most of it stems from these righteous middle lane drivers. Those in the outside lane find there's no room to move in and the situation feeds on itself. Within a short time, irate drivers break the law by passing obstructors on the inside and danger escalates rapidly.

Note the word *quickly* in the second rule. Another factor which chokes these roads is the overtaker who won't use his best turn of speed, who appears deliberately to take "forever" to overhaul whatever he is passing. Again, unless their car has little power, it is probably the "I have a right" mentality . . . When their speed is unusually slow, relative to normal speeds in an outer lane, this can be a part cause of rear-end collisions. It is the knock-on effect back down the traffic queue build-up that is so dangerous, even though when accidents result we cannot excuse the drivers there. Far from having any "right", the middle lane hog is either driving blissfully unaware of the problems he is generating behind, or simply "without reasonable consideration for other road users".

To the fast driver overtaking in the outside lane, a full middle lane, which should not be, is a cause of danger in itself. At the stage a middle lane vehicle is being directly passed, safe speed in the outside lane, especially in bad weather conditions, has to be less because the safety margin of space all around is that much reduced.

On our crowded roads and motorways, slowing down for safety in this situation – even though you will still be going fast – can mean you suddenly find drivers behind you have closed up dangerously. They shouldn't, but they do. For that to happen when the middle lane is in proper use is bad enough, without it happening through selfishness.

The rush-hour periods when bus lanes are restricted for other drivers are usually short and well signposted. Nevertheless, too many drivers bunch up into the other lanes rather than read the notices. You can promote traffic moving freely by using bus lanes properly.

Lane discipline must extend to where lanes are *not* painted. Examples include going around roundabouts; at the mouths of junctions; on country crossroads; etc., etc. At these places divide the road into lanes in your mind's eye and position accordingly. Drivers who selfishly straddle what could be two lanes cause endless hold-ups. Using first class lane discipline is infectious and makes the roads safer. Do it.

'ROAD JUNCTIONS: TURNING RIGHT: TURNING LEFT: ROUNDABOUTS'

Please study the rules in each of these sections of your Code before this book continues with its deeper analysis of selected ones.

The STOP sign means STOP – by law. Regardless of need you must STOP, even if for only a second. You move on only when you have checked all ways from your stopped position and know that it is still, or is now, safe. If you fail to STOP, your examiner will fail you. He has no choice if you break a law.

In Situation Two of Lesson 4 we noted how priority normally lies with drivers on the major road. What does "Approach junctions with great care" mean therefore, from their point of view? It means slowing down for ALL junctions, controlling speed until you see if there is anyone there waiting to emerge, and if there is, holding back until you are sure they have seen you and will wait for you to pass. It's easy to re-accelerate when all is well but hard to stop when it's not.

To restrain speed in this disciplined way depends upon your scanning ahead towards every junction becoming a habitual and deliberate part of looking where you are going. Staring blankly ahead is not enough. You have to make your eyes work to focus on key points where trouble may arise.

Those who tear past blind turnings in the belief that no one ever comes out of them without looking, can be almost certain of being made to think again. The driver most prone to accidents is the one who makes no allowance for other people's mistakes!

Ahead you see a vehicle starting to cross your major road. Unconcerned you continue, neither reducing speed, nor even covering your brake pedal with your foot as a precaution. At this point, that driver stalls half way over. Had you merely eased off your accelerator in the first place and covered the brake you could have stopped gently, safely. It would have cost so little; now you have an emergency on your hands mainly of your own making! On all such occasions good drivers instinctively cut speed and cover their brake until their eyes confirm the other driver will get clear. You never know if his engine is cold, or about to break down, or if he will just make a mistake.

Suppose as a learner you are the one to stall. Calmly, quickly use the recovery procedure of Lesson 2. If the engine will not go, then with the clutch up in 1st gear, turn the starter. The battery should propel you the short distance needed to reach safety. But think and look round first. Battery-powered reverse might be the better option. (Unfortunately, with automatic transmission the battery cannot be used in this way.)

At many junctions, vision from the side turning is unusually restricted because of hills, badly parked vans, etc., etc. It is vital that when you are clear to pull out of such a turning you do so extra smartly. Major road drivers come fast. Pitifully few ease off as I have just advised. To protect you further wherever a stall could prove lethal, reduce your risk of stalling by using double your normal moving away acceleration – use as much as you would starting on a steep hill.

The Highway Code says elsewhere that the flashing of headlamps must only be used like the horn – to alert someone you are there. If, while you are waiting at a junction, you see another driver flash his headlamps you need to be wary that that is all he means. Customs which won't lie down existed long before the Code rule was drafted in an attempt to prevent confusion. There are still lots of drivers about who will flash at a junction to say "You drive on, I will wait". Others flash on the opposite basis to warn "Stay where you are, I'm coming through". And a flash might be intended for someone else rather than you! With such scope for muddle you must make no assumptions. Judge a driver by his positioning and by whether he has stopped or is moving, not by his flash. And beware the headlamp flasher who, having apparently encouraged you forwards, suddenly decides to go himself.

At a traffic light the coming on of amber with red still means STOP. You can prepare to go but you must not move, or creep one inch, until the light turns green. Even though green changes the priority, it still may not be safe to move. The most immediate possibility will be of pedestrians still brushing past your bonnet. Situation Six of Lesson 4 highlighted other potential dangers too.

Referring to ALL junctions, the Code says "Drive on only when . . . you will not block the junction." This rule applies to major road drivers just as much as to a driver emerging from a minor road. It applies to ALL junctions not just to box junctions, where the yellow criss-cross patterns have had to be painted because so many traffic jams otherwise result from foolish driving. Wherever there is a major-road hold-up you will nearly always see drivers in it move up in the queue oblivious of their blocking off a side street. Because there may be no one waiting immediately to turn into or out of the side street is no excuse. Can't they think ahead that someone may come while they sit there?

In the same way, selfish drivers move on to a roundabout even though they can see their own exit is jammed. Traffic destined for other directions cannot then pass through; and, hey presto! a jam on one exit mushrooms into a mega-blockage for all routes. You must avoid this thoughtlessness for others.

"TURNING RIGHT" – Please look back at figs. 13 and 14 to remind yourself of right turn traffic priorities before referring to fig. 21 and the text below.

As you approach your turn, aim to position your car, running just to the left of the centre line from about a dozen car lengths out. Visualise a centre line if none is marked.

There may be times when such problems as road works or a badly parked car result in oncoming traffic encroaching

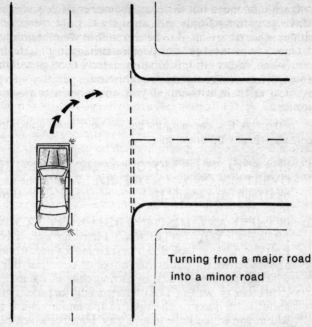

Turning from a major road
into a minor road

Fig.   21

your side over the centre line. In this event you dare not
move over as much as usual. Scan your eyes ahead, not just
for the erring driver crossing that line but for any *reason* that
one might try it by the time you get there. You can then
position accordingly less far over.

All this planning has to start a very long way ahead if you
are to arrive at the junction correctly positioned, speed
under control in 2nd gear, ready to turn immediately, or
wait, giving way to oncoming traffic. Your instructor will
help you judge the timing of each factor.

Regular mirrors' discipline should mean you are aware of
the extent of traffic behind before you decide to make the
turn. Your first step is nevertheless to consult the mirrors
once more. Then you signal and keep a weather eye
thereafter to ensure that drivers behind have seen your
signal.

Once safe, move out to your left-of-centre-line position. Make your move firmly, not abruptly but not tentatively either; other drivers need to be clear about your intentions.

Once you have taken your position driving just inside the centre line, stick to it. It is important that as you slow right down, drivers from behind can begin to filter past to your left as soon as there is room. If you wander you can cause accidents.

In the last few car lengths before your turn you must consider three vital questions:-

1. IS A CYCLIST OR MOTORCYCLIST TRYING TO OVERTAKE ON YOUR OFFSIDE? Whether he may be at fault is irrelevant! He is too vulnerable not to allow to go first.
2. IS THERE ANYTHING IN THE MINOR ROAD TO PREVENT YOU ENTERING? First check, is it No Entry? After that look down the turning for pedestrians about to cross, traffic obstructions or whatever, anything which might stop you from getting clear of the major road in one movement. Look out especially for pedestrians about to step across the neck of the minor road – to whom you would have to give way. Hazards which can lead to your being stuck with the back half of the car still blocking the major road can be very dangerous.
3. WILL THERE BE A SUFFICIENT GAP IN THE ONCOMING TRAFFIC FOR YOU TO MAKE YOUR TURN WITHOUT A STOP – AND WITHOUT CAUSING ANYONE TO SLOW DOWN?

Reaching the turn itself, your speed should be down to barely moving. If the three questions have raised no problems, don't stop. Go on smartly but do not cut the corner. Follow the path shown in fig. 21. That car illustrates the correct waiting position but the path it takes is the same as you must follow even when no stop is needed. Up to that waiting point you do not turn your steering: a) because safety demands you keep inside the centre line until going; b) because if you are hit from behind, you don't want to be buffeted round into more danger.

If you have to stop at the point shown in fig. 21 apply the handbrake and select neutral. To stop forward of that position is wrong because the turn then becomes impossibly tight. While you wait for your chance to go, continue to scan your mirrors as well as repeating the three questions. Look for trouble before it finds you! Check your indicator is still on.

At the first clear opportunity to go, use the normal GET READY and MOVE AWAY technique of Lesson 3. Confidence with your footwork when you gain experience will mean you can plan to move at the precise instant your gap comes free. But you mustn't creep forward ahead of that moment, causing yourself the tight turn warned against above. A rapid glance over your shoulder as your car starts turning can help you protect a reckless motorcyclist racing up your outside, unaware of your plans. If you get amongst several right turners, take your turn in the queue with the same attention to every detail.

If a car awaits turning right from the minor road of fig. 21 (positioned like the car in fig. 22) theoretically you can ignore it. Being on the major road you have priority. If it is a crossroads, the same applies vis-à-vis someone emerging from your left to cross over. You have precedence over everyone except oncoming traffic. You can't however, rely on others to stick to the rules. Greedy and ignorant drivers often creep forward from a side road and compromise your safety. (Right turners who cross a centre line before they should are much the same.) Should a rule-breaker make your position dangerous you may have to abandon your plans. When one creeps in front of you let him go. Anger is dangerous at the wheel.

In fig. 22 the driver does not have priority. The Give Way markings across the end of his street confirm the major road status of the other road. Those broken lines may be the sole marking denoting precedence. Towards the end of the minor road there may be added a 'Distance to Give Way line' sign, or a full GIVE WAY sign, or a large white triangle painted across the carriageway, or there may be none of these. Usually it is the bigger or more dangerous junctions that have the extra signing. Whichever Give Way marks may have been used, they mean *let major-road traffic go first*. Remember that at a STOP signed position you MUST stop. At a Give Way

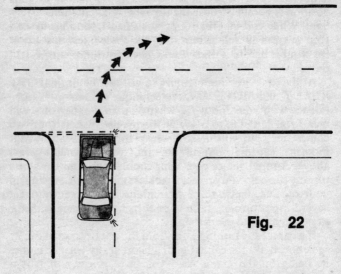

Fig. 22

Emerging from a minor road into a major road

position you can go on without stopping provided there is no one to Give Way to. If there is or you can't yet see, you STOP.

Other than at very open Give Ways which are seen to be clear sufficiently far *in both directions* as you come up to them, you will find that you almost always have to stop at the Give Way line.

Up to that point your technique – getting into the right position next to the centre line early (taking account of traffic behind), getting down into 2nd gear and so on – should be identical to that just described for the right turn into a minor road. By correct positioning you help left-turning traffic from behind you to go on if there is room and if it is safe, even though *you* may have to stop. If you fail to hug the centre line you will block them and cause unnecessary annoyance. Having said that, if the mouth of the minor road is narrow you will unavoidably block left-turning traffic behind. In these circumstances you must also consider the chance of a lorry or coach wanting to turn right or left INTO your minor road while you are there. If you position yourself too close to the centre line at the entrance, any such large vehicle may be unable to get round into the road. Stop just left of the normal position instead. To begin with, your instructor should advise before you reach it if he thinks a road end narrow enough to need special positioning.

Years ago children grew up with a simple safety dictum for junctions and for crossing the road, "Look right, left, and right again". Unfortunately the Green Cross Code ousted that saying from their lips. The children's road death toll has risen ever since. Your instructor should already have introduced (or re-introduced) the slogan to you for safety at junctions. But you need more:-

1. You must check the major road pavements from the moment they open up to view during the last yards before you stop. To see why, imagine an extreme example where high hedges at the end of the minor road conceal children about to 'burst' across from one side to the other, trying to catch their dog.

2. Just before your stopping point you must look to your immediate front and sides for anyone who may swing into your minor road too fast. They may be making a wide left turn, or cutting across your bows in a right turn. Wrong though they may be, unless you are awake and pull up sharp you can have a bad smash.

3. When you are having to stop, never whizz up to the line frightening people as to whether you will stop. Stop gently, with your front bumper up to the line to command the best view both ways. When vision is restricted take the last bonnet length or so barely moving so you cannot frighten the type of moped rider who zooms past absurdly close.

4. In the final seconds of drawing up at the line, your slogan look R, L, and R again should already be at work. The first look should always be to the right (unless you are entering a one-way street coming from your left) because that is where traffic closest to your nose will be coming

from. At a minimum you must work the slogan TWICE–
even if the road appears clear and you intend no stop.

5. When you do stop, continue looking R, L, and R
    repeatedly until you see suitable gaps in the traffic from
    both directions becoming available simultaneously for
    you to make your right turn.

Why at least TWICE in 4. above? Because your eyes have an
in-built blind spot, car design creates more with the door
pillars, and rain or smudges on the windows also mask the
view. You must look each way long enough to register
movement across these blind spots despite your instinctively
moving your head to compensate for them. Cyclists remain
hidden easily but believe me, a lorry can be missed if you look
too quickly. Inefficient looking is a prime accident cause.

To start with, your instructor will guide on how long a gap
you need to pull out safely. Being in 2nd as you reach the line
means you are prepared for going on if it is safe to go at once
without any stop. An examiner will be pleased to see any safe
opportunity made use of. Most times, however, you need to
stop, apply the handbrake and come out of gear to neutral.
You then have to anticipate when the next safe gaps both ways
will coincide, so that you can have your clutch up at the biting
point and your handbrake held up with the button in, ready to
go the very second those gaps open up. You shouldn't take
gear or begin raising the clutch until a moment or two
beforehand (as noted in Lesson 4, page 72) but this prudent
anticipation enables you to make the necessary smart getaway
in safety. It also avoids the irritation of drivers behind who
hoot when they see opportunities lost by those amateurs who
only start to prepare when gaps are upon them. Should the
prospective gaps fail to materialise, return to neutral and
release the clutch until you see another chance in the offing.

Had the car in fig. 22 been emerging at a CROSSROADS,
all the same applies. We will deal with someone opposite
waiting to turn right in a moment. If they are waiting to come
straight over, remember you will have to give way to them in
the middle, before you can turn. *Note* that straight-over traffic
should normally take a "left laned" approach position but
that they can choose a "right laned" approach if traffic, road

layout or signs make that more appropriate.

At crossroads when you turn right, the principal rule says ". . . where there is an oncoming vehicle also turning right, drive your vehicle so that you keep it to your right and pass behind it (offside to offside) . . .". The rule applies whether you are turning OFF, or ON, to a major road, as well as at traffic lights. Fig. 23 shows this basic right turn procedure.

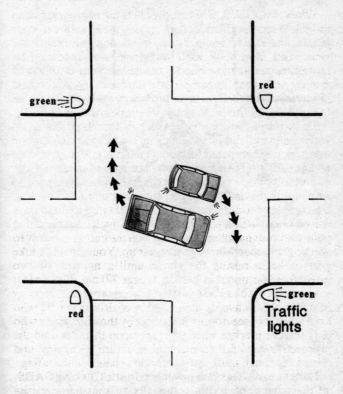

BOTH CARS TURNING RIGHT

Fig. 23

Unfortunately there are junctions without enough room to pass offside to offside. Fig. 24 shows how you are then allowed to pass in front of each other (nearside to nearside). Lines and arrows on the road are often used to make this exception into the rule at a particular junction or lights. The change is usually made official because of lack of space but occasionally it's done to speed up traffic flow in one or other direction.

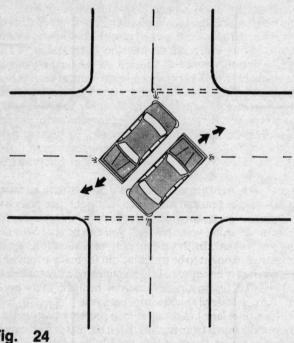

Fig.   24

Extra care is vital when passing in front. You have a much restricted view of traffic (especially two wheeled traffic) coming from behind the other car. (Remember you must give way to them as you will be crossing their path.) This is why it is the exception rather than the rule. Unfortunately, more and more people are doing it as a matter of course when they should be using the basic right turn procedure of fig. 23.

At first you must rely on your instructor's guidance on which method to adopt at busy crossroads, as well as on how to interpret what other drivers are likely to do. Unless the other driver's positioning gives away his intention you may have to wait 'til he moves. The main danger is of being forced to stop astride a crossroads because of muddle. You could both be hit by major-road drivers going too fast who presumed you would both get clear. That those drivers would be blameworthy too (see page 113) is little recompense.

The basic rules extend to dual carriageways. When turning off one you first plan your way over to the right hand lane in good time. When you reach the junction you make use of any filter lane and then position yourself on the farthest side of the turn-space, which is provided in the central reservation to insulate you from fast through-traffic. You can wait there safely, if necessary, before crossing the other half of the dual carriageway. This correct positioning allows room for anyone turning right from the opposite direction, or turning right from the road you are heading for, or crossing straight over the dual carriageway, to make use of his part of that protected turn-space.

Signal your right turn well ahead – about twice as far as normal – so that you can move into that right lane early. As you begin to slow down keep a wary eye in your mirrors for any lunatic catching you up so fast you can be sure he is not seeing your signal. In this admittedly rare situation, which your instructor ought to be watching out for ready to advise if necessary, it may be better to forget your plans early enough to speed up out of his way, rather than risk being hit in the boot. Then move in (safely!) and let him pass you.

Where a filter lane has been made to protect you from such types, get well into it from its start. Even normal drivers expect you to get out of their way as quickly as possible. If the turn-space (and its filter lane, if provided) is full and you are thus forced to stop initially in the right hand lane of the dual carriageway, leave a long gap between you and the person waiting in front. This applies particularly if you are among the first few drivers thus exposed to fast traffic from behind. If our lunatic does appear in the mirrors, at least you then have some distance to move up as he slithers towards your boot.

When you reach the junction be prepared to wait first at the end of a filter lane until you can get across to your correct turning position on the farthest side of the turn-space. Never block the nearer half of the gap which, as I have explained, is for use by others. And don't be tempted to sit on it just because it may be empty when you arrive; someone will always turn up and then you could be a cause of danger. Although as the major-road driver it could be argued you have priority over anyone from the side road(s), this is a case of consideration for others. In any event, you would potentially be blocking anyone turning right from the opposite dual carriageway direction, over whom you would not enjoy priority in the nearer half. However, if there is no filter lane, rather than wait with your boot exposed, you may need to move on to that nearer half of the turn-space despite the possibility of someone more entitled to use it, arriving. It depends whether specific danger to your boot warrants it but if you do, at least anyone arriving sees you established there and can alter their plans accordingly.

As with non dual carriageway junctions, you may also have to contend with passing in front (see page 122), either because arrows on the road command it, or when given no choice due to other drivers' actions or a narrow layout.

"TURNING LEFT" – First we examine turning left into a minor road as in fig. 25. Check your mirrors specifically and begin signalling about 50 metres (50–55 yards) before your turning. (If there is risk of confusion with some prior turning, you have to delay the signal.) Your instructor will guide your precise timing on the first few occasions and help you judge your speed reduction and gear changing down to 2nd.

You need 2nd by six to eight car lengths before the turn and walking speed by the time you reach the position in fig. 25. Slow speed here is vital.

If your speed happens to have been low enough, you can drop direct from 4th to 2nd (or it might be 5th to 3rd at an earlier stage) but it's best not to make this a habit. Examiners could view it as lazy car control.

Your slow speed enables you to look well down the minor road before you turn in. Pedestrians may be there to give way to, or some obstruction on your side which will mean a temporary wait before you can pass it, or perhaps there will be

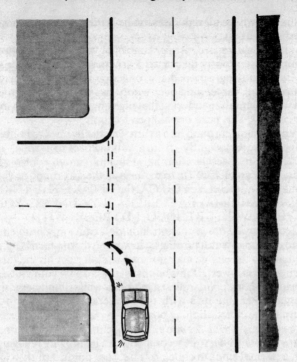

Turning OFF a major road.

Fig. 25

a daft cyclist cruising up towards you on your side, hands on his head! If you wonder why I place so much emphasis on LOOKING WHERE YOU ARE GOING at turns, it is because learners so often forget, whenever they have a mass of other new things to think about.

Slow speed as you reach the turning allows time to double-check your mirrors for anyone on two wheels trying to squeeze through on your nearside and time for a quick glance over your left shoulder to make sure. If there is a cyclist there, hold back, let him go. The Code warns you never to overtake a cyclist just before you make a turn. Cutting across him could easily throw him off balance even if you don't hit him. Never assume he will be all right because he is turning; he may hope to go straight on.

Without slow speed, proper control of your car for the turn is impossible. Poorly instructed learners swing into turnings too fast, straying on to the wrong side of the road, tyres complaining, car leaning over wildly swaying on its springs, and with themselves suffering that nightmare feeling of having lost control. This need not happen to you!

When you steer round into a turn you ideally need to be able to accelerate *very* slightly – from a walking pace to a stride – at most. This tiny acceleration harnesses maximum control. It means you can tuck well in to the kerb all the way round as you should. OBVIOUSLY, YOU CANNOT TAKE THE TURN UNDER (MINIMAL) ACCELERATION UNLESS YOU HAVE SLOWED UP ENOUGH TO BEGIN WITH.

Getting speed down enough shouldn't cause any problems at most normal-width turnings. However, where a turn is tight and narrow the engine may threaten to stall right on the turn when speed is lowest. If this happens, press down your clutch, only to the biting point for just a moment, while simultaneously raising the engine revs with the accelerator. You can thus return to the clutch slipping position – as learned in Lesson 3, page 56 – *but from on the move*. Taking clutch slipping control means that within a split second you can be moving on again with a normal smooth clutch release. (Do not just push your clutch down beyond the biting point. That disconnects the transmission. You would then be 'coasting' under momentum without full control. Coasting is incorrect under any circumstances.)

The above technique needs practice in a quiet location before you will be able to do it without a second thought. Ultimately you will learn how to slow down smoothly for a turn, dropping speed sufficiently for the crucial stage, but without laying yourself open to charges of dawdling either before or after it. Increasing skill will mean you rarely need to resort to clutch slip except say, where you have had to hold back a fraction, mid-turn, for a pedestrian to cross.

Turning left INTO a major road involves most of the same techniques as you learned a few paragraphs ago for turning right on to one. The important difference is that you tuck well in to the left on approach as shown in fig. 26. You must keep

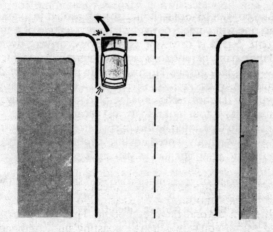

Turning INTO a major road.

Fig. 26

tucked in when you come to steer round too – a wide sweep is a bad fault.

Added Safety Tips For Turns

1. There are times, especially at night, when you need to shift your bottom forward in your seat to see properly both ways before you dare emerge at a junction. To make sure that door pillars, etc. cannot be obstructing your view, move your head back and forth as well. "Fairly sure" is not good enough. Never depend on your instructor's or anyone else's judgment. Look for yourself.

2. Your final glance, made as you draw out into a major road to go left or right, should normally be to the right, where traffic on your side of the road comes from. (BUT, see 3. below!) However, at many Give Way points you can see further one way along the road you want to join, than the other. The direction with the more restricted view is nearly always the one from which trouble springs unexpectedly. Therefore, keep an eye in *that* direction instead as you begin to move forward, even if it happens to be to the *left*.

3. As you wait to join it, it may seem reasonable to assume no one will come from your left *on your side* of a major road. NEVER drive on assumptions; drivers overtake dangerously at junctions putting themselves on your side of the road, despite Highway Code rules. One of these ruthless drivers could swish close past the line just as your bumper reaches it. Never be tempted to start putting your nose out without looking left, just because you are clear to the right. One could be lurking in a stream of left-to-right traffic you thought need not affect your left turn, and pull out on to your side just as you emerge.

4. If the throat of your minor road is narrow and high walls or hedges restrict the view either way, you need to inch forward until you can see. Such tricky spots often have a STOP sign to comply with first. As in 2. above, look in the direction with the shortest view as you edge forward. Your instructor must advise how far to allow your bonnet to penetrate the road as you try to see enough. On one street corner in a thousand, despite your inching out, the view remains so restricted he would have to tell you when you had edged out to such an extent that a quick getaway before anything could come was now the only appropriate thing. It often helps to open your window. A car can usually be heard coming before you see it, although unfortunately the same doesn't apply to a push bike.

5. Once on to your major road, build up speed quickly. Check your mirrors straightaway. To find someone there already should come as no surprise in these fast-driving days despite their absence as you pulled out.

"ROUNDABOUTS" – To decide in which lane to approach a roundabout, think of it as a glorified crossroads and select the lane you would use if that were the case. It will be the same for a "mini" roundabout as for one the size of a stadium. If you plan to turn left, use the left lane. To turn right, take the right hand lane. For straight ahead you can pre-select either lane or a middle one, depending on traffic flow. Make your decision early and stick to it even if an error means taking a direction you don't want and having to find the way back to your own route later. Don't dither, or attempt to chop and change. Learn to plan further ahead. If white road-arrows designate a specific lane for your destination, use it.

Where there are no lane lines on the approach, or going round the roundabout, fill them in in your mind's eye. By sticking to a 'lane discipline', you help other drivers to assess your intentions and you make room for greater traffic flow.

Signals for roundabouts are set out in the Code. Arm signals are inappropriate. Start signalling well before taking your chosen approach lane. To get directly over to the innermost lane on the roundabout, you may have to cross several marked *or assumed* roundabout lanes in the process. As each of these roundabout lanes is on your right you must give way to anyone already in one of them. When you come to leave the roundabout and have to cross the same several lanes to reach your exit, you will be indicating left. That, you might think, should warn other drivers to let you across – your being on their right. Unfortunately, such consideration is rare despite the Highway Code and the rules. In practice, you must be eagle-eyed, both with your mirrors and an occasional rapid over-the-shoulder glance to confirm what they tell, and prepared to wait (or go round again) if others won't let you over to go off.

Third gear may be appropriate for a vast traffic-free roundabout. For the rest, 2nd is essential to give flexibility so you can stop or move on as situations develop. For your first few roundabouts, reckon on having to stop at the entry-point, use the handbrake, and move on in 1st when safe. With greater experience you will be able to judge those times when it is safe to merge in with the flow of traffic without stopping. You 'time' your final approach accordingly, slowing down as needed, or making use of an instant burst of power in 2nd, so as to slip effortlessly into a safe gap and on your way.

Changing lane on the way round a roundabout often depends on good timing too. You slip to your lane ahead of or behind a driver already in it – always within the rules on priority – by first slowing a fraction, or after a brief touch of your accelerator in that responsive 2nd gear.

You need lots of practice on roundabouts, simple ones to start with, tough ones later. When learners bungle roundabouts it is usually because they are insufficiently sharp-eyed. They don't see cyclists or motorcyclists, especially the sorts who circle around the outside edge. They don't make those essential pre-lane change, over-the-shoulder glances. Or they spend too long looking behind and don't spot that the car in front has stopped! Need I repeat LOOK WHERE YOU ARE GOING first, foremost, always.

I said earlier NEVER drive on assumptions. Imagine a learner stops behind another car at the Give Way entry-point to a roundabout. He sees that a gap in the roundabout traffic will soon become available and prepares to go. Excited as the gap quickly becomes a reality, he starts to move, still looking to his right. Bang! The driver waiting in front didn't move! Perhaps he thought the gap too small, perhaps he fell asleep! It doesn't matter. The learner's assumption that he was bound to go ahead too was flawed. "To ASSUME is to make an ASS of U and ME"!

The relief of having a gap materialise, after a long wait to join a busy roundabout, is another trap for learners. Having been looking exclusively to the right whilst waiting, they start to move before noticing that the first exit to the left is blocked, and waiting vehicles have stretched right back to just in front of them; they also fail to look towards the pavements for pedestrians setting out to weave across between cars. Watch you don't fall into such traps.

ONE-WAY AND GYRATORY SYSTEMS – Should you ever miss the NO ENTRY sign at the exit of a one-way street or system, plenty of clues soon alert you: parked cars on both sides all face you; arrows on the road point towards you; back-to-front road signs seem hard to read, etc. Stop. Put on your hazard warning lights until ready to move. Then ask your instructor to back the car out of danger unless you have sufficient reversing experience to do it under his guidance.

In a narrow one-lane one-way street beware of jay-walkers and carelessly opened car doors from BOTH sides. Many such streets are designated play-streets by the children who live there; whether the Law agrees and puts up relevant signs or not is irrelevant. You must not race down these one-ways even if they are splendid short cuts. That's the sort of speeding that kills.

Wider one-ways need to be split into lanes. Visualise them if none are marked. Choose your correct exit lane early but unless it is a very short one-way street you need not fret to get into it at once. For example, where your street joins a one-way street it might abut the right hand lane of that one-way. Suppose you know you want to turn left a few hundred yards along the one-way. If, at the time you reach the one-way, the right hand lane is clear, enter it even if the left lane is full and you can't yet move directly over to it. Drive on in the right hand lane and pick your chance to transfer later. If you wait for the left lane of the one-way to come free before you even join it, you simply hold up everyone behind you unnecessarily. You would only need to wait for a chance to get into the left lane straightaway if your proposed left turn exit happened to be almost immediately after your point of entry. The same concepts apply if you join a one-way in its left lane with a view to making a right turn in due course.

In a right hand lane, as well as expecting to be passed on your left, increased alertness to extra danger arising from your close proximity to the right hand pavement (as in the narrow one-way mentioned just now) is vital.

Turn right from a one-way street from the righthandmost lane. Never attempt it from the wrong lane. Equally you mustn't indulge in the opposite sin, if you are turning left and have failed to transfer correctly to the lefthandmost lane. Go where your 'wrong' lane takes you. Sort out how to get back to your route later.

Having pointed out you need not always change lanes (if you need to) immediately you join a one-way street, I should explain that you should always grab an opportunity to cross to a clear lane, even though it may arise long before you really need it. That is far better than leaving it too late! You would rarely wait until the last moment and then only if there was no alternative. In that event, you would have to choose between pulling up in the lane you were in and waiting calmly until someone let you go in front of them, or missing your turning. If people behind you in your present lane will be held up, sometimes the honourable thing is to miss your turn and sort yourself out later. Were it to happen on Test, you would wait rather than miss the turning your examiner had requested, unless he issued a fresh instruction.

The right moment to change lanes therefore is a matter of prudent timing. Normally, you signal early and merge into the lane you require, using the same timing skill for changing lanes that we met on roundabouts a few pages ago. A glance over your shoulder to pin-point someone's exact position and speed can help decisions a lot. Provided slipping into a lane comfortably ahead of someone travelling at the same speed as you are doesn't cause him any need to slow down, that's fine. A 'mini' burst of acceleration in low gear will often clinch it safely, fairly. But where a person is gaining on you, you mustn't cut in on him. Slow down for a gap further behind, or if you've plenty of distance before you must change, keep going; wait a while for a better opportunity. In heavier traffic there may be few gaps to go for; even though you are signalling, the considerate driver who makes a gap is all too rare. Fortunately, your instructor will be there to advise on the handling of difficult circumstances in line with the *general aim*, which is to avoid complete stops. Unnecessary stops can clog the traffic flow which a one-way exists to promote. Only if everyone drives helpfully, as well as skilfully, on them can they fulfil that prime function.

All this lane-changing advice assumes you are still LOOK-ING WHERE YOU ARE GOING, watching out that neither the traffic in front of you, nor the vehicles in the lane you are trying to join, are pulling up on you. The second of these can make the gap you head for disappear without trace!

Gyratory one-way traffic flow schemes, like vast stretched roundabouts where several trunk routes converge, can have six lanes or more for you to contend with as you go round. To cross several lanes, tackle them one at a time, if necessary, but never miss an opportunity to switch several at once. Look out for white painted lane direction arrows which have to be followed, like it or not! It's not just a matter of seeking the arrow for your direction; you may have to be quick to change out of a lane headed elsewhere. But this concentration on your destination mustn't divert your attention from pelican crossing lights turning against you, other drivers cutting in in front of you and so forth. Many such systems are town centre schemes where dozy shoppers mill about the road protected only by your wide-awake driving.

In a middle gyratory lane, traffic passing you on both sides at once can be disconcerting. You may prefer to choose a right or left outside lane where possible, so as to have people passing on one side only. A kerbside crowded by parked vehicles or thronged with people can more than counteract the benefit, however, and you still have the possibility of two-wheeled traffic trying to squeeze between you and the pavement. The choice must therefore depend on the road conditions.

SPEED LIMITS – The main limits in the Highway Code you must know are the ones for cars. Each applies *nationwide* for its defined category of road EXCEPT where a different higher or lower limit is signposted. The thing to know is that the national limits apply everywhere – signposted or not; whereas a changed limit can only apply where repeater signs (on lamp posts, etc.) carrying a black number in a red circle define what it is. The end of a special limit is marked by the 'national speed limit applies' sign or a different speed restriction sign as appropriate.

GIVE BOOK BACK TO INSTRUCTOR

JOINT REVIEW AND ASSESSMENT

Like Lesson 4, this lesson needs questions on it to be asked of your pupil, having had a look through it yourself. Together with questions he is sure to have, that will open out the whole subject sufficiently for you to make sure you can cover any weaknesses, without forgetting to show how pleased you are with what he has absorbed correctly. The Department of Transport produce a helpful booklet in addition to the Highway Code, called 'Know Your Traffic Signs'. Though it's not strictly necessary for the Test, I thoroughly recommend having one. Old hands can benefit from it as much as learners.

The quiz below completes this lesson. When you agree the date for Lesson 8, add to your Progress Chart (if necessary) anything that's going to need a refresher by then.

HIGHWAY CODEBREAKER

1. Q. List as many actions as you can which require use of the Code routine: Mirrors – Signal – Manoeuvre beforehand.
    A. Overtake, turn, move off, change lane, slow down, stop.

2. Q. How is a built-up area defined for speed limit purposes?
    A. In simple terms it is anywhere with street lighting.

3. Q. When turning right at a crossroads on to a dual carriageway, on which side of the central reservation turn-space might you wait if necessary?
    A. Normally the left, unless road markings dictate otherwise. Remember, the right hand half needs to be kept free for people opposite or for anyone coming from your left wanting to turn right off the dual carriageway. However sometimes, particularly at T-junctions rather than crossroads, local layout and custom precludes taking a strictly correct position and an instructor must advise from experience.

4. Q. What sign will you see on a bollard in the middle of a one-way street?
    A. A blue circle with a pair of white arrows both pointing down, but with the arrowheads split apart to show that you may pass either side of the bollard.

5. Q. What is the difference between a one-way traffic sign and a one-way street sign?
    A. The first is repeated along the street to remind drivers. It has a white arrow on an oblong blue background and is pointed upwards. The second is displayed horizontally, facing streets that are joining the one-way, to advise incoming drivers that it is

one-way and in which direction it flows. The sign is similar, with the words one-way added.

6. Q. Describe the sign which tells all traffic to turn right. Where might you find it?

A. Horizontal white arrow pointing right on blue circular background. Typically found at traffic lights at convergence leading into gyratory system.

7. Q. Name and describe the sign which shares its shape with none other.

A. STOP. Written in white on a red octagonal background.

8. Q. Emerging on to a major road to turn right or go across, should you move half way out if there is no traffic from the right although you are still waiting for a gap in a stream coming from the left?

A. Normally no. But where getting out of a turning can be very difficult if you don't, you will see other drivers do this on the reasonable basis that if they are established sitting there before anyone new appears from their right, although that person will have to accept having to stop for them, they will not then be a cause of that person having to slow down suddenly. You need to see the technique used safely to learn what to do if you ever need it. There will be times when driving along a major road that you come across someone "established" in this way. Remember you have no right-of-way (see page 78); they could hardly give way to you before you were around! Slow down; then wait if you have to.

9. Q. When can you pass a STOP sign?

A. After you have STOPPED at the line and checked all ways.

10. Q. What is the basic rule for a box junction?

A. You must not enter the box if your exit road or lane from it is not clear unless you are turning right and expecting to be held up on the junction (if at all) only by ordinary traffic priorities.

11. Q. Why are all traffic lights to be treated as box

junctions whether or not yellow criss-cross lines denote them as such?

A. The rule at traffic lights is "Do not go forward when the traffic lights are green unless there is room for you to clear the junction safely". Commonsense decrees that if you expect the lights to change shortly it is pointless to move forward on green when a queue on the far side is going to leave you stranded in the middle. You will only risk obstructing the crossing traffic. The red light then puts the legality of completing the manoeuvre in doubt too.

12. Q. Into which lane should you join a dual carriageway?

A. The left lane. Turning left onto one, this causes no problem. When turning right (via the central reservation turn-space) it *can* do, if the left lane is constantly full and therefore difficult to move directly across to. The common practice in this event is to choose carefully a moment when the right lane is clear *for a very long way*, and set off smartly in it, using it like a filter lane to gain speed until you can merge over to the left lane, or else carry on because you then have more vehicles in that lane to overtake. I say "common practice" because the Code gives no specific advice on this. It therefore can only be done strictly within the Highway Code Commands on page 75.

LESSON 8

LIGHT TRAFFIC

OBJECTIVES

For your learner to be able to cope in light traffic with: moving away – gear changing – arm signals – turning corners – giving way at junctions – negotiating roundabouts – proper positioning – observing traffic signs – stopping.

LOCATION and DURATION

This lesson is intended to be repeated on a variety of routes within built-up areas but NOT for a city or town centre and NOT, on the first occasion, on a wet day. Your learner is not ready for those extra difficulties. In between the repeat sessions, reversing can be introduced from Lesson 9, provided your learner completes the home study part of it first. The two types of lesson can then intermingle until you are *both* happy about all-round competence. You should then be ready for the toughest conditions of town traffic in Lesson 10. Remember, an hour at the wheel is enough for most learners.

When you do come to practise in wet weather, please first refer to FURTHER PRACTICE on page 141.

INSTRUCTOR NOTES

Plan each route you want to use in an area you know. An individual route should take 12–15 minutes to drive and include at least one roundabout, some crossroads and a mixture of right and left turns both into and out of minor roads. Circuits are best. They have the advantages of being easily memorable and of being gone round again to iron out mistakes.

Provided it does not interfere with his concentration, encourage your pupil when he's at the wheel to tell you what he is doing and about to do and why – and to ask EARLY if he is in any doubt. This gives you an insight into his thinking and helps you appreciate the reasons for errors. He may lack knowledge or he may harbour misconceptions about things you thought he knew. Be friendly and responsive so that he can feel secure in the knowledge that you always want him to ask questions in good time, as you have said.

Be ready to caution or advise. The speed with which a learner's difficulties can escalate on early drives can shock you if you've never instructed before. Look out for:-

1. Little concept of what is a safe speed.
2. No idea of appropriate following distances (especially as a learner).
3. Still less judgment of when to slow down or stop.
4. Looking exclusively at the kerb in order to steer some set distance away from it, instead of looking where he is going

and just aiming the car there.
5.   Worse than 4, steering solely on the basis of trying to miss oncoming traffic, to the exclusion of seeing any other danger.
6.   Weaving about the road (often a clue that 4. or 5. is happening).
7.   Fixing eyes hypnotically on back of the car ahead.
8.   No appreciation of positioning or speed control in relation to jay-walkers, parked vehicle doors about to open, cyclists about to detour round man-hole covers, etc. – if these potential dangers are even recognised as such.

All these are common learning problems, not stupidity. If any persist beyond a lesson or two, adopt the inquiring approach I have suggested to discover the causes; you should soon put them right.

BRIEFING

Before you set off, review your Progress Chart as required.
Explain how every learner needs to return to this lesson several times, over differing routes, in order to reach a high standard. On this first run of the lesson you will drive round the whole of a chosen route two or three times to start with, demonstrating the objectives. The amount of demonstration necessary when you come to different routes later, will naturally reduce. This time, during part of your demonstration, you will want him to concentrate on observing your exact positioning in the road at every moment, and on recognising how you are constantly relating speed to the ever-changing conditions. You will challenge him to prompt you at once when he sees a need to adjust speed or position. If he doesn't tell you far enough ahead, you will intervene to make the comment yourself. Make this interplay competitive if you can, without letting it distract your driving; it will sharpen his awareness.

LESSON PLAN

STAGE 1 – On the way there and as you drive around your first planned route for demonstration purposes, point out the distance you maintain from the kerb, how early and how much you move out to pass parked vehicles, how you drop speed at once if stopping becomes necessary, and so on. Work in any specific demonstrations of particular objectives of the lesson you feel your pupil may need.

STAGE 2 – Going round the route for a second time, remind your learner of your challenge in the Briefing. Ask him to "instruct" you on every change of positioning and/or speed you need to make. Say where you are going but leave him to suggest: "prepare to move out to pass that cyclist . . ."; "enter the filter lane provided here . . ."; "slow down, that lorry has started backing into the carriageway . . ."; etc.

Suspend his "instructions" a moment if a chance comes up to show something new. For example, a safe opportunity to overtake offers you a "live" example on which to point out all the factors you take into account. Or you may need to toot the horn to warn someone on foot you are there, and want to explain why it needs to be done at just the right moment.

STAGE 3 – Drive round your circuit once more, this time having your learner "talk you through" as many additional aspects as he can think of, e.g. – pointing out who has priority – when to signal – where to be looking when – road signs to obey – interpretation of other drivers' actions, etc., etc. Resist jumping in with your own comments before he has a chance! Far better for him to suggest a mistake now, than to MAKE it later!

STAGE 4 – Now he is familiar with the route, ask your learner to drive round it. There shouldn't be any need to give route directions but remind him in good time if he looks like losing his way. Remember to suggest he keeps you posted on everything he's doing, so far as time allows, and on how he is thinking ahead, planning his every move.

Watch closely his reactions to other traffic. If he is not responding to other drivers' signals (or lack of them!), or to changes in their speed or positioning in a developing situation of increasing danger, be ready to instruct decisively before a crisis occurs. But avoid premature and perhaps unnecessary concern turning into a talk-through.

STAGE 5 – Back at the start of the circuit, your learner will probably appreciate a break while you discuss any major misdeeds. Then he may enjoy driving the circuit once or twice more. Pull him up before you reach any spot where he made a mistake last time around. Then you can discuss what happened and how it should have been handled. Unless the fault related to other traffic, you are then ready for a (corrected) action-replay.

STAGE 6 – Another break will not go amiss. First miles are exhausting. If your learner has been coping well, see if he would like to branch off onto other lightly-used roads for a short while, or perhaps drive round the first circuit in the opposite direction. Otherwise go round the same circuit one more time. This time ask him "What is behind you?", "What road sign did you just pass?" and similar questions. Tell him you will be repeating such questions until he never fails to know the answers without guessing or having to check the mirrors.

STAGE 7 – To complete the first time out on this lesson, your learner might drive home or perhaps part-way there. You must judge both the suitability of the roads and whether progress justifies it. How far he should drive will also depend on how fresh he is. The hour or so at the wheel already will be enough for most, even with the breaks, especially after the initial instructing beforehand. If you do decide he can drive home, watch carefully for tiredness setting in. Even if he doesn't drive home today, most learners reach the stage during the repeats of this lesson, when you are happy for them to be driving to and from home.

ASSESSMENT

At home it will be valuable to "re-run" the lesson together, "street by street" so that you can present him with the usual checklist of things to think about, and update your Progress Chart at the same time. Be generous with your praise and encouragement; his first experience of driving in traffic, however amateurish, is a major achievement.

FURTHER PRACTICE

You cannot give your learner too much practice. Extra lessons all build up confidence and awareness towards other road users.

If you need to go out on a wet day, jump to the start of Lesson 10 for a few moments together, before going. Discuss all the Emergency Stop advice there. Although it's early days for your learner to have to cope himself with an Emergency Stop in the wet, he needs to have a good understanding of how much harder it is to stop on a wet road. Demonstrate a couple of Emergency Stops before your learner drives, so that he appreciates the reality of wet surface problems and increased stopping distances. Apart from the above, I have reserved any direct teaching of the full Emergency Stop until reversing and manoeuvres have consolidated the learner's 'feel' for car control. However, you may judge that your pupil is ready to begin practising them earlier. If so, let him try. But for most learners, Lesson 10 will be soon enough.

Before fixing the time for each additional lesson on a different route, consider aspects of his driving still needing improvement. Make sure HE understands what he must do to get them 100% right next time. Dispense with your own initial demonstrations except to introduce things missed out earlier: perhaps no chance has yet arisen to overtake; or you now want to show how a 5th gear is used; or you are ready to bring in using arm signals; maybe you need to show "live" the technique for regaining clutch control on the move when negotiating an unusually sharp turning.

With regard to arm signals, concentrate on times when a "slow down" signal should be used and how to give it clearly at just the right moment. (See page 77.) Explain that a right or left arm signal is only ever used *in addition* to the indicator (unless it is being given because the indicator has failed). In case he is asked for them during part of the driven stage of his Test, your learner should practise them as well, though you can leave this to a later stage if you prefer. Discuss how such a signal normally need only be given once, decisively and long enough to be seen, as you slow down for a turn. Because both hands must be on the wheel during the turn, it mustn't be left too late; nor can it be given while changing gear, or no hands would be on the wheel! As a right or left arm signal implies slowing down, you *don't* give a "slow down" signal as well. The action for a turning-left arm signal must be instantly distinguishable from a "slow down" one. If you have to wait at traffic lights, etc., you repeat a turning signal briefly before moving off. If you are the front vehicle having to wait where a traffic controller is on point duty, you can help him by adding, while waiting, the appropriate signal given in the Code.

ADDITIONAL HOME STUDY

Between repeats of this lesson, your learner should return to the Highway Code and study the rules for *non*-drivers – 'The Road User on Foot', 'Extra Rules For Cyclists', 'The Road User In Charge Of Animals', etc., so he knows what to expect from them on the road. He must also know the drivers' rules on breakdowns, level crossings, driving in fog, and accidents; and he should look at the sections on 'Vehicle Security' and 'First Aid'. The 'Law's Demands' listed in the Code enforce many of these rules, so he also needs to study what he hasn't already seen there.

The following quiz should be fun to give at an appropriate time.

HIGHWAY CODEBREAKER

1.   Q. Should a cyclist ride in your slipstream?
     A. In the Code, No. In life, he will. Watch for him.

2.   Q. How might an inexperienced cyclist negotiate a roundabout?
     A. By going round exclusively in the left hand lane or getting off to walk.

3.   Q. What should those first to come across a road accident do?
     A. * Warn the next traffic to arrive, if safely possible – with hazard lights, red triangles, traffic cones, waving down (from a position you can't get hit).
        * Ban smoking . . . switch engines off . . . arrange to summon emergency services.
        * Remove casualties only if in immediate danger, not unnecessarily.
        * Give first aid . . . get uninjured people to safety.
        * Stay and reassure until emergency services arrive.

4.   Q. What hazards might you watch for particularly,
        when you see holiday-makers climbing out of their
        car?
     A. Children or dogs escaping into the road.

5.   Q. Driving at night along a road with a footpath on
        the right hand side, where should you expect a
        pedestrian going in your direction to walk?
     A. On your side with his back to you! You needn't
        worry about the ones correctly on the footpath; you
        must be prepared for the idiots.

6.   Q. When a train hits a car there are rarely any
        survivors from the car. Name the five main things
        you should never do at level crossings.
     A. Never drive over nose-to-tail. Never move on to the
        crossing unless there is space to get off it on the other
        side. Never stop on a crossing, or just beyond one.
        Never zig-zag around the barriers.

7.   Q. If your car breaks down, what should be your
        immediate priorities?
     A. Remove car from road if you can. See that you and
        your passengers stay out of danger too, and don't
        stand obscuring hazard warning lights if they need to
        be on. Warn other traffic as in A.3. above. Keep side
        lights on at night or if visibility is bad. There is more
        to consider when you break down on a motorway.
        Read the motorway breakdown section in your
        Code.

LESSON 9

REVERSING

OBJECTIVES
For your learner to be able to reverse:-

1. Straight.
2. Round into a limited opening.
3. For the three point turn.
4. Into a roadside parking space.

LOCATION and DURATION

The reversing practice needs exceptionally quiet level streets. The three point turn requires about 25 feet (7–8 metres) width between pavements. Half-an-hour at a time is usually more than enough for reversing, which is why I suggested you could bring the subject progressively in amongst repeat sessions of Lesson 8.

All that is needed before you can do that is about half-an-hour's home study. However, if you do split this lesson down, I would urge you to keep to the order of stages in the Lesson Plan (from page 153) in which the skills are built up in a deliberate progression. Once all the objectives have been attempted, each skill can be practised individually to perfect technique as required.

HAND THIS BOOK TO YOUR LEARNER

HOME STUDY

One of the first things you learned was basic mastery of the clutch. In Lesson 7 you added how to regain clutch slipping control on the move (page 126) which I hope you have been able to try out in Lesson 8. All this footwork, combined with use of the handbrake, is identical in reverse. Successful reverse manoeuvres depend on clutch control of every degree of speed, from barely perceptible movement to a stroll. (Above that, your clutch would be right up.)

Steering movements in reversing are the same as for forwards with one difference; your upper body is turned around.

ALWAYS START BY PULLING THE STEERING WHEEL DOWN ON THE SIDE YOU WANT TO GO

Imagine looking down on the car from above and relate that to fig. 27.

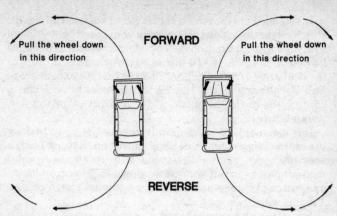

Fig. 27

REVERSING SINS

We have all witnessed the menace who daily backs out of his driveway, too idle to do the obviously safer thing – reverse IN, and drive OUT forwards. The Code condemns such practice. It also warns you about children hidden below sight while you are reversing. They can be particularly at risk in a driveway. If in the slightest doubt about children, get out and check or have someone outside guide you back. It is for such reasons and because control is more difficult that it is against the law to reverse further than necessary. I would add: never reverse faster than you can walk.

REVERSING STRAIGHT

You need to begin your reversing on a straight, EMPTY road with clear pavements – perhaps a quiet lane or a cul-de-sac. Strangely, it is by steering a wobbly course first that you discover how to steer a dead straight one! A few repetitions of reversing very slowly back about 50 metres (50–55 yards) or so, weaving from one side to the other, quickly teaches you to which side the back of the car responds to your steering movements. Because thereafter you will know at once which way to turn the wheel for a steering correction, you will find you can reverse in a good straight line with no problems.

If you need only reverse a car length or so, you can slip the clutch all the way. You can maintain your speed below that of a racing tortoise purely on clutch pedal movement as taught in Lesson 3, page 56. If you intend to reverse several times as far, you can go a bit faster once you have some experience of how the steering reacts. Having set off under smooth clutch control, you can let the clutch right up and drive at up to a slow walking pace.

It is invaluable to know exactly how slowly you can drive the car in reverse without needing clutch slip. Reverse being a very low gear, you can let speed drop to almost-stopped without having to put your clutch down to prevent stalling – and still be able to re-accelerate later without kangaroo hops. Try this with your instructor.

For reversing you must turn well round in your seat towards the centre of the car so as to look out of the BACK and the rear side windows. You must reckon to give way to *everyone* else who may appear, from whatever direction. (Stop and wait, if necessary pulling in to the kerb first.) The absence of "front-view" mirrors therefore obliges you, as you progress, to make frequent glances back round out of the FRONT to see 'behind'! However, once on the move in reverse, you must LOOK (BACKWARDS) WHERE YOU ARE GOING most of all. Keep both hands on the steering wheel all the time.

REVERSING INTO A LIMITED OPENING

On this Test manoeuvre you are asked, after backing in to start with, to continue to back slowly, keeping in a straight line, reasonably close to the kerb for some distance. For a left hand reverse, you start from two to three car lengths beyond a suitable quiet street corner. Then reverse round the pavement edge keeping no more than two feet (just over half a metre) out. Once straightened up, you keep reversing at the same distance out until the examiner asks you to stop. If it's a right hand reverse you start similarly next to a right hand kerb and street corner. Back in on the same basis. Then continue reversing as for the left side reverse at the same distance out, but this time it is from the offside (right hand) pavement. When it comes to moving away again after the reverse this side, you need to adapt your safe move-off routine and return to the left hand side of the street straightaway. If you are too close to the mouth of the junction, you may need to reverse further back before you can do that safely.

You are responsible for pulling in safely to your start position. If there is someone waiting to come out of the street as you arrive for a left reverse, you may need to delay using your left indicator and pull in further beyond the turning than would be ideal. Otherwise, that driver could well assume you were going to go left down the street in the ordinary way, and pull straight out! Before pulling over prior to a right hand reverse, position and give way to approaching traffic just as you would if turning right off a major road. If you have to wait next to the centre line, stop noticeably beyond the street corner but leaving yourself enough distance to move across to the starting position you want.

There is no official guidance on indicators for these Test reverses. Nevertheless, I suggest you always keep the appropriate indicator on as you back round, to help make your intentions immediately obvious.

You are only asked for one of these reverses on Test. We'll concentrate first on the left reverse being the one thought more difficult and therefore more commonly tested. The numbered items below are matched by the arrow numbers in fig. 28. They highlight what you must think about at each stage. How slowly you must control the car and how far from the kerb you need to be, follows no. 7.

1. Look all round (including in front – not just behind); wait until you can move without affecting other traffic.
2. Look down the turning. Be prepared to wait or move forward if another car wants to come out.
3. Double check the major road both ways. Check pavements for children etc. Be aware that your front wing will swing out as you turn.
4. Begin to turn very gently, slightly earlier than you might expect. After one more yard or so (or one metre) put elbow grease into steering rapidly to take you round.
5. Start straightening up. Be quick about it or you'll turn on too far – into the kerb.
6. Check all directions and all pavements again.
7. Continue in reverse, parallel to the kerb, until told to stop. Keep looking backwards but don't forget sufficient

glances round for dangers looming to the sides and out front.

Your start position should be the normal 6″ to 9″ (15cm–23cm) from the edge. By number 2/3 you need to have eased out to two feet (just over half a metre) off the kerb. Keep to that on the way round and as you reverse further back. Under clutch control in steps 1 to 3, speed can match the racing tortoise; but in 4 and 5 it must be cut to that of an arthritic snail. That is the maximum that will allow you enough time to steer accurately.

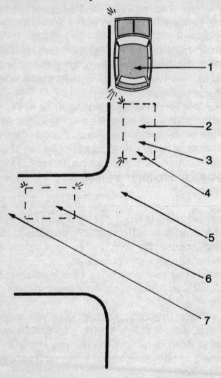

REVERSING THE CAR INTO A LIMITED OPENING

Fig. 28

Fully straightened up in 7, you can bring your clutch up fully and increase your pace to (backwards) walking speed.

The right hand reverse has the advantage that during 4/5 you can check directly over your right shoulder the exact proximity of the kerb. However, you should revert to turning inwards to look through the back window as soon as possible. You are then more likely to notice other traffic, children playing, etc.

THREE POINT TURN

On Test, you will be asked to turn your car in the road in the sequence shown by fig. 29. Try not to let the car wheels touch the kerb on either side; however, you probably wouldn't fail just for one gentle nudge – provided you put things right without panic. In a very restricted width, your car may need to overhang the pavements slightly as each side is reached but that mustn't be by enough to endanger or obstruct any pedestrians present. Ideally, you take three moves but an examiner will not fail you just because you take five – or even seven. What he really wants, is to see your control of the car and your care for other road users.

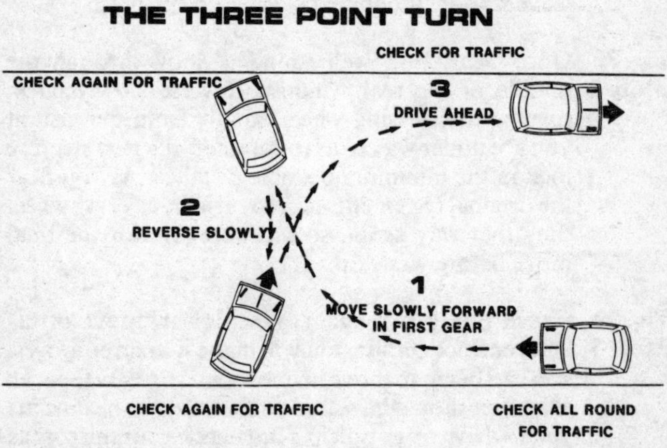

THE THREE POINT TURN

CHECK FOR TRAFFIC

CHECK AGAIN FOR TRAFFIC

3
DRIVE AHEAD

2
REVERSE SLOWLY

1
MOVE SLOWLY FORWARD
IN FIRST GEAR

CHECK AGAIN FOR TRAFFIC

CHECK ALL ROUND
FOR TRAFFIC

Fig. 29

Some roads have pronounced camber. They dip sharply towards the gutters. This means that after you stop at each kerb a "mini" hill start is needed. Near the edges, rapid steering is required to gain the optimum steering angle before you cross the main part of the road. The very short distance in which all the steering must take place (2–3 feet or $\frac{1}{2}$–1 metre, for each direction change), demands clutch slipping control of your speed to that of our friend the arthritic snail while it is done. You can go a little faster across the middle of the road but it's not a race! To avoid unacceptable strain on the steering parts, you only turn the steering from the instant the car moves.

Before you start, double check the road is clear ahead and behind. Then:-

Fig. 29 Arthritic snail speed and energetic steering movements
Move 1 must achieve full lock (wheel turned as far as it will go) within the first 2–3 feet or $\frac{1}{2}$–1 metre moved. Just before you stop at the opposite kerb, whisk the wheel back the other way ready for Move 2.

Before 2, check both ways. Wait for vehicles to pass unless they clearly intend to wait for you. The Highway Code forbids waving people through so leave it to their choice.

Fig. 29 Once clear, turn well round to look through the
Move 2 middle of the rear window. Reverse slowly back, turning the steering wheel rapidly from the instant you are under way so as to complete the new steering lock in the minimum possible distance. As you near the original pavement, start to turn the steering wheel the other way again, so as to prepare for the final move before you stop.

Fig. 29 Check both ways again. When clear, move off as
Move 3 before. Once certain you will make it in three moves, you can begin to move on more smartly. (By then, an examiner should have told you whether he next wants you to drive on or pull in.) But check your mirrors as you come out of the turn; if someone wants to pass, you may need to keep in while they go.

During each of the three moves you should have time, as you move across the middle, for long-range glances in both directions to forewarn you of anyone coming.

PARKING BETWEEN CARS

Although not required on Test, this important manoeuvre is worth learning properly. This book advises your instructor to use chalk marks on the road and plastic dustbins for your first attempts. It will be much safer, and possibly cheaper!

Most vehicles can easily be reversed into a space one-and-a-half times their own length. Start with one which is twice your car's length. Practice and experience will enable you to achieve the tighter manoeuvre. Success depends on arthritic snail speed, especially as you change steering locks.

Fig. 30 shows the manoeuvre for a space on the left. (Normally you would only use a space on the offside in a one-way street but this book will have to leave it to your instructor to show you the small differences.)

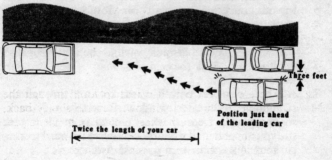

Three feet

Position just ahead
of the leading car

Twice the length of your car

PARKING

Fig. 30

Here is the sequence:-
1. Having spied your parking space well ahead, check for other traffic to ensure you will not cause an undue obstruction as you pull up, out in the road just beyond it. Use your left indicator to signal your intention. (Keep it on until you are in.)

2. Pull up adjacent to, but with your boot slightly ahead of, the boot of the next car beyond the space, about three feet (one metre) out from it.
3. Turn round in your seat to gain the best view through the middle of the rear window and the passenger side window. Reverse slowly back until almost level with the other vehicle. Check again for traffic (from both directions). Your front wing is going to swing out as you turn in. If that could endanger people passing by, you must wait accordingly.
4. Looking backwards again, begin to reverse gently in, turning your steering progressively leftwards so as to *aim at the mid-point* of the exposed kerb.
5. When your back bumper is about to overhang the kerb begin turning the steering wheel back into full right-hand lock. Watch that your left front wing will miss the car in front; once clear, put on the remaining right-hand lock rapidly. This should bring you round parallel to, and close to, the pavement.
6. In your concern not to bash your front wing, remember you are moving backwards so you must mainly be LOOKING BACKWARDS! Pedestrians from either side will try to squeeze between you and the vehicle behind, whether you think they must be mad or not, you dare not squash them.
7. Just before you are parallel to the kerb and 'in', begin to straighten up the steering. Aim to stop a foot (30cm) or so (not less!) from the car behind. Complete your straightening up in the course of moving forward so as to park equidistant between the other two vehicles.

You are now ready to start going backwards!

HAND BOOK BACK TO INSTRUCTOR FIRST

PREPARATION

Check through your Progress Chart before the driving practice. Find a straight "no-through-road" over 50 metres (55 yards) long with no parked vehicles, or the nearest equivalent you can. Choose a quiet time of the day too. If it is wet you will first have to introduce your trainee to the extra potential problems involved unless you have already. See page 141.

When he first begins reversing, your learner may easily overlook other vehicles or pedestrians. Be ready to stop him soon enough. Then he can look and see what he should have seen.

LESSON PLAN

STAGE 1 – Your learner can drive to the practice area if you can find a suitably quiet route there. Reverse the car a short way back into your straight "cul-de-sac" for him, stopping well out from the kerb, provided no traffic has appeared.

STAGE 2 – Ask him to reverse back to an agreed point towards the bottom end of the road under clutch control, never exceeding the speed of an athletic tortoise. Have him turn towards the centre of the car to look out of the back window, and watch that he keeps both hands on the wheel without crossing them. Encourage him to steer the car gently from side to side on the way, to get the 'feel' of what happens when steering in reverse. Make sure he keeps checking for other road users, especially kids on bikes, etc. But keep your own eyes open too. When he stops, be ready in case he forgets to apply the handbrake and select neutral before asking questions.

STAGE 3 – Discuss any problems. Then repeat the exercise.

STAGE 4 – Repeat the exercise a little faster and for a greater distance. Ask your learner to begin under clutch control but to bring his foot completely off the clutch once under way (just as in forward driving). He must still keep below walking pace, now controlling speed entirely on the accelerator. Again, keep him steering left and right as he goes. Watch for other traffic yourself all the time; if he doesn't react to any problem or ask at once what to do, you must step in and advise before danger can arise.

STAGE 5 – After a short rest he should be ready to reverse the car a good 50 metres (55 yards) back down the road in a straight line. From his home study and having seen how the back of the car reacts to the steering wheel, he should find that the small "corrections" required to keep the car straight are easily mastered. The first attempt can be shorter, under clutch control with the car barely moving. If that is good, he can then repeat the exercise over the full distance, this time at a walking pace, controlling speed on the accelerator.

STAGE 6 – Repeat the straight line reverse, this time having him move into and out of clutch slipping control (as learned in Lesson 7) when you instruct him to speed up or slow down.

STAGE 7 – Let your learner drive to a street you select for "reversing into a limited opening on the left". Ask him to pull in to the kerb just beyond the opening and switch off the engine. Ask him to describe the reverse manoeuvre in detail so you can be sure he knows exactly what is expected.

STAGE 8 – On his first attempt you will need to talk him through stage by stage. If he misjudges the steering, make him stop, get out (watch he remembers handbrake, neutral, etc.) and see for himself exactly how much too close, or too far out, the car is. Then he must drive forward, back to the start point, try again – and inspect again if need be.

When he gets the steering RIGHT, stop him in the middle so that he can inspect *that*. This getting out will be the quickest way for him to learn to relate what he sees from the driving seat with what happens outside.

Six attempts should be enough for one session. By the last, I hope you will only need to say "Well done!". In repeat lessons introduce the right hand reverse.

STAGE 9 – Your learner can drive on to find a quiet street with no "through-traffic" for the three point turn. You need one of about 25 feet (7–8 metres) width. From describing the manoeuvre himself beforehand (based on his home study), follow the same teaching process as for the reverse turn above. Half a dozen tries will be enough.

Talk him through his first attempt. Insist he gets out to see if he is close enough to the kerb when he stops at either side. For success, lock-to-lock steering changes must be completed within a total of 2–3 feet (½–1 metre) of forwards or backwards movement. You may need to demonstrate how vigorously the steering wheel has to be turned to achieve this. Unless your learner can, at will, hold speed on the clutch to that of an arthritic snail, he won't be able to manage the steering tightly enough; you will have to go back to perfecting his clutch work.

STAGE 10 – Your learner can drive home via the same quiet route. The last objective of this lesson is to park safely between cars. If there is somewhere near home where you can do so, draw two chalk marks on the road as shown in fig. 31.

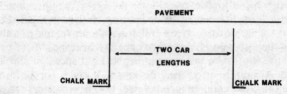

Fig. 31

Position an empty plastic dustbin or a similar, easily seen, hittable object to represent a car, in the angle of each mark. Before he starts, make sure your learner can talk *you* through every step he intends to take. He can now practise in relative safety until he achieves a perfect "park" without touching the dustbins. As with all manoeuvres, getting out to look for himself – how near the wing is to the dustbin, etc. – will help enormously. But watch out that he doesn't forget to have eyes everywhere for other road users. In future lessons he can park 'for real' once you are sure your paintwork will survive!

NOTE
While I strongly recommend the "dustbin" system, if there is nowhere to do it, the manoeuvre is best left until later after more experience. The thing to do then is find a suitable parking spot twice the length of your car and for YOU to demonstrate the manoeuvre before your learner attempts it.

When you show him, remember you risk scratching other people's expensive cars. Try not to hit them! Talk your learner through, the first time he tries.

ASSESSMENT
After the lesson, discuss progress against objectives. Update your Progress Chart.

FURTHER PRACTICE
In future lessons as you continue to practise these manoeuvres, carry them out on hills, progressing to steeper ones as technique improves. Use sharper – "more limited" – openings, narrower streets and so on. The Test won't be so demanding but knowledge he can cope whatever the terrain, provides your learner with proof of his competence and does wonders for confidence.

Before doing that, you will need to teach him how backing a short distance down a steep hill towards an opening, and similar such situations, sometimes need to be done simply by easing the footbrake but continuing to hold speed in check with it. Although speed may never rise enough for you to release the clutch and engage reverse, you nevertheless must have your clutch down, with reverse selected, to be ready to feed in engine braking or acceleration as required.

LESSON 10

TOWN TRAFFIC

OBJECTIVE
For your learner to be able to drive competently through busy town traffic. The lesson concentrates on:-
1. Stopping in an emergency.
2. Anticipation of other road users' actions.
3. Planning ahead.

DURATION and LOCATION

About thirty minutes of home study is intended to come before the first session of driving. The lesson is designed for approximately one hour at the wheel. The whole lesson, or parts of it needing extra work, can be repeated at will and blended into continuing driving practice up to the Test.

To start with, Emergency Stops must ONLY be practised on *dry*, wide, quiet, straight roads away from parked cars. When your learner is more experienced they must also be done in the wet. The other conditions above are then even more important.

Try not to use a rush-hour for the first attempt at town driving. Your learner can work up to that.

HAND THIS BOOK TO YOUR LEARNER

EMERGENCY STOPS

Before you drive in a busy town or on wet roads, you must know how to stop in an emergency. Ideally, you should never have to do so through your own misjudgment. You will be consistently:

* thinking ahead and looking for possible danger
* driving at a safe speed for traffic and road surface conditions
* slowing down and/or braking early *before* any hazard becomes a crisis.

Total perfection is impossible. We ALL make mistakes. The day will come when you have to make an Emergency Stop despite everything. Your Test therefore includes an Emergency Stop. The examiner calls for it at an appropriate moment unless an unexpected real emergency arises first. (He always gives a rough idea beforehand of when it will be.) This ensures that no driver receives a full licence without having had instruction and practice in stopping in an emergency.

How otherwise could you cope at a place offering no chance to swerve with, say, a child running out only a few car lengths in front of you? The child's life over-rides all other considerations – even fear of the car behind crashing into your rear. That ought not to happen if he is following at a safe distance.

However, if it does, both he and you are strapped inside protective boxes. The child is defenceless.

Later in this lesson, your first Emergency Stop or two will be a re-play of the Quick-Reaction Stop you learned in Lesson 3, rather than a full Emergency Stop. Thereafter you will learn to reduce your stopping distances until you can match, both on wet and dry roads, those of an experienced driver.

Your instructor will standardise with you a pre-arranged signal for each stop. He will probably say "Stop!" accompanied by a tap on the dashboard with his hand, which is the same sort of signal the examiner normally arranges with you.

When the command is given, your instructor (or an examiner) will have checked all round, including behind. You don't worry about your mirrors. You just STOP as fast as you can.

A full Emergency Stop is not an exercise in stamping the brake and then clutch pedals to the floor as hard as possible. That would probably produce a dramatic skid. On a wet or skiddy surface, violent skid might be a better description.

You have to apply the footbrake not just quickly and firmly but *progressively* under control. The examiner will not expect you to allow the manoeuvre to develop into a real emergency. As in normal stopping, you only press down the clutch pedal a moment or so before the car stops. This ensures that you benefit from any engine braking that can be helping you.

WHAT TO DO IF YOU SKID DURING EMERGENCY BRAKING

Because there will always be skids where it is impossible to restore control in time, they are frightening. However, they are less worrying once you understand how to counteract them instantly.

A skidding road wheel is described as 'locked'; that is, it has stopped turning and is sliding; once doing so it cannot be steered. Your wheels will lock on a wet road more than twice as easily as on the dry. Anti-lock braking systems, now being fitted to more and more cars, are set virtually to solve the wheel-locking problem. Meanwhile, less sophisticated braking systems are still in the majority, so we will look at them first.

The most common cause of skidding is excessively hard

braking, either in relation to speed, or during cornering, or against available grip on a wet or slippery road. Suddenly your road wheels are locked instead of rolling; and steering response has vanished. You may hear the "hiss" of the wheels sliding on a damp surface or you will experience the familiar terrifying "screech" where the road is dry. Unless they are rolling, only a small patch of each tyre gets into contact with the road. The braking achievable by such a small area of rubber is minuscule. Normally the rolling wheel is continuously renewing that patch with fresh tread to work against the road surface. Getting your wheels rolling again to kill the skid is therefore crucial.

To do this fast with an ordinary braking system you must:-

1. Instantly ease your footbrake pressure by about half. With luck, you should at once find that your wheels roll, steering response returns, and some braking is restored.

2. (A). No sooner than you have eased your foot, it must go back down like lightning to restore maximum braking, BUT THIS TIME it must be at a fraction less pressure than the level which resulted in the skid. As no one can precisely judge that level in the heat of an emergency, you have to use an on/off-when-they-slide repeating technique – a controlled pumping action – to achieve the best braking you can. In theory this best braking is achieved by consistently braking to the point of locking the wheels, without them ever actually doing so.

2. (B). From the moment steering response reappears in no. 1 above, you may, simultaneously with your braking recovery action, have to seize the chance to prevent the car trying to spin round. Such a spin would begin with the back wheels starting to skid away to one side. You must quickly "steer into the skid" by turning the steering wheel in the same direction as the back wheels are sliding. Instantly the slide stops, steer straight again. Hopefully you can follow at once by steering to recover your course, or at least out of danger. If you find yourself rolling backwards having spun round, get the brake on before you hit something!

2. (C). Thankfully, spins are rare. Your *normal* emergency steering reaction, which must match your lightning-fast footwork, is to get the steering straight if it isn't already.

This lets the front wheels, which account for around 80% of stopping power, roll more easily, and means they can apply more braking to the road before they will lock.

I hope you can now see why braking should be complete BEFORE you reach a bend. If you skid on a bend, your recovery chances, with the added leverage of centrifugal force working against you, are slim.

ANTI-LOCKING BRAKES

Soon most new cars will have anti-lock braking systems. Electronic sensors monitor the instant any wheel locks during emergency braking and trigger an immediate brake pressure reduction to the wheel concerned. Thereafter for as long as the driver has his foot hard on the brake, the most brake pressure that wheel can cope with (short of locking), is maintained throughout the emergency. To hold that maximum, the slightest change at the road wheel gets tracked by the sensors. A compensating increase or decrease in the pressure is made within a flash. A shift from a wet to a dry surface might be an example. Each wheel is controlled independently. For example, three could be braking normally whilst the fourth sorts out a skid on a patch of oil. Or, all four could be under simultaneous 'computer-control' but working at different pressures.

Anti-lock brakes thus stop you in emergency in a straight, or practically straight, line without skidding. Overall stopping distances are reduced as a bonus. You simply push hard on the brake. The system takes over. A major advantage is that because the front wheels will not even lock on wet roads, you retain steering control. This means you can still steer in the midst of maximum emergency braking. That could be crucial. Suppose you had to brake and simultaneously steer round a child who had fallen off his tricycle. With ordinary rather than anti-lock brakes you might have to sacrifice maximum braking for critical split-seconds, so as to get the front wheels rolling and a chance to steer clear. Time you may not have.

KEEP AWAKE IN EMERGENCY

When you practise Emergency Stops, your instructor will not allow you to get into a severe skid. But one day, no matter how good your brakes are, you are certain to have one. So get hold of this:- in a real emergency it is no good if you simply jam on the brakes and "freeze" – waiting to skid into an accident. Your lightning-fast brake reaction must include instantaneously countering any wheel locking, or developing spin, as explained above. But you must think fast as well. What other vehicles or pedestrians are near you? Can you safely squeeze past an obstruction with an inch to spare? Might your horn and lights alert a vehicle or pedestrian quick-witted enough to move out of the way? If it's a question of hitting a child or a dog, hit the dog! etc., etc.

ANTICIPATION

Consistently safe driving is not just a matter of luck. A good driver thinks ahead and ANTICIPATES the POSSIBILITY of a hazard before it arises. Some tips below should start you on the right lines.

PEDESTRIANS

- Watch for hurrying shoppers stepping into the road without looking. They are especially prone to jettison road-sense during severe cold or when there's a downpour.
- Watch children near schools, playgrounds or pedestrian crossings. Don't expect them to behave like adults!
- Watch beneath parked vehicles for moving feet.
- Be ready to stop halfway round blind corners on country lanes. ANTICIPATE a herd of cows, or fallen trees, etc., blocking the road. *Assume trouble until you see there's none*.
- Watch for passengers jumping off moving buses, not just at bus stops.
- Be prepared for bus drivers who pull out from bus stops as if they owned the road. Although the Highway Code asks you to give way to them after they start to signal if you safely can, that does not bless them with priority. However, a good many bus drivers seem to believe it does! Also expect bus drivers to stop for passengers without pulling in – baulked by badly parked vehicles, or too lazy to use a specially set-aside bus stop area.

CYCLISTS

- Cyclists are especially vulnerable when they take up position prior to turning right. Give them an extra wide

berth. That lets people behind you see them out near the middle of the road earlier too. If you are coming the other way, stop if you can and allow such a cyclist to get clear. Use a slow-down arm signal too if possible.
- When you see children on bicycles ANTICIPATE impulsive or dangerous behaviour as well as failure to use signals.
- ANTICIPATE a cyclist ahead of you pulling out to pass a pothole. If he's coming the other way and has the same problem, a motorist about to overtake him by a normal berth could suddenly swerve right into your side of the road . . .

MOTORISTS
- If you are paying attention to traffic lights or a junction you will soon reach, you can often ANTICIPATE the driver ahead braking before you see his brake lights. Be prepared for him to change lanes without warning.
- Take note of 'L' plates and expect impromptu stops.
- Watch for the driver with the uncancelled indicator. ANTICIPATE that he may not turn at all or that he might suddenly turn in *either* direction.
- Watch out for the driver who abruptly pulls in for sweets or a paper when he spies a corner shop. Or the one who suddenly remembers he needs petrol and practically skids in to the forecourt. These 'impulse' drivers are more dangerous than the ditherers; at least the latter make themselves obvious.

PLANNING AHEAD
Your own actions must be constantly planned ahead:

TRAFFIC LIGHTS
How should you adjust your speed when approaching a traffic light where you intend going straight on? Lights which are green when you first sight them often change to red by the time you reach them. Slow down sufficiently to make stopping easy if they do change. If the lights are red when first seen you should both slow your speed and get down into 2nd gear. You are then prepared if they change through red and amber and to green before you reach them, to drive on without stopping,

subject to the way being clear.

Suppose the light phasing is unusually short. Green turns to amber when you are across the line or too close to it to stop without having to brake dangerously hard, risking an accident. Amber means STOP but in this circumstance the Highway Code accepts that you may have to go on. However, you must watch for the driver who leaps away against the red-and-amber light that will, by then, be showing in the other direction. There is a real risk of an accident. In Court you would both be on dubious ground. Probably you (for going too fast in the first place) more than he.

JUNCTIONS

Before you reach ANY junction you must plan to be: AT THE RIGHT SPEED – IN THE RIGHT LANE – IN THE RIGHT GEAR. As soon as you see one ahead, raise your foot off the accelerator. That way, speed will be falling off to give you time while you work out what you may have to do: mirrors, signal, gears, lane change, etc. You avoid last-minute decisions. You can always speed up again if the opportunity arises.

Suppose you are flowing along a suburban road into town. There is only one lane your side and you want to turn right or left at a traffic light or a junction not far ahead. To turn right, position yourself at the right hand edge of that lane immediately left of the centre of the road. To turn left, you tuck in well to the left of it. Then if you have to stop you won't be sitting straddling the middle of the lane. Doing that would stop motorcycles, etc. filtering past you. Quite often it stops cars too, where a better positioned driver could have made room for all.

Where several lanes become available to you (roads are often widened out at junctions), look for white arrows on the road and/or destination marks, such as A69, T'N C'TRE, etc. Take your correct lane or the most appropriate one as soon as possible. Remember mirrors and signal before changing lanes.

STOPPING DISTANCES AND FOLLOWING DISTANCES

"Never drive so fast that you cannot stop well within the distance you can see to be clear." Half the driving you see, openly flouts this rule. The way drivers ignore it when there is bunching ahead of them defies belief, especially on motorways. The master driver abides without fail by this Highway Code dictum. He knows you cannot stop dead on a dry road whatever false belief or car salesmen may promise! He knows that stopping distances extend out of all proportion to increases in speed. He knows how immense is the self-discipline required to stop yourself straying outside the rule during good road conditions. He is also aware that extending your margins 3–4 times on wet roads, or obeying the Code fog rules you learned earlier, or respecting the possibility of black ice, each call for realistic restriction of speed with an even greater strength of character.

To avoid accidents demands effective speed-management. Suppose a lone car appears in the opposite direction when you are doing 60 mph on a flat, dry, straight, wide, and otherwise empty, single carriageway country road. At the point where you will pass each other you will only have half the road width at your disposal for several moments. Self-discipline dictates that you ease your foot off the accelerator until he has gone. Why? Either of you could suffer a sudden tyre burst; he might fall asleep and wander towards you; no list can do justice to the baffling variety of things that do happen – just occasionally. Later on the same journey, you notice a horserider's hat behind a hedge ahead and you see a gate beyond that. You immediately slow down on the basis the horse might bolt for the gate despite a sensible rider's intentions. If it does, you can then stop without panic. Otherwise once you see it is safe you can re-accelerate.

Far-fetched? Not at all! It is the sort of skilled observation that distinguishes the master driver from the good driver. The master manages his speed in accordance with the slimmest chance of what MIGHT happen – not merely what he sees. Going up over the brow of a hill on a trunk road he slows and extends his following distance behind anyone in front; he expects to find a traffic jam the other side until he sees there isn't one. A car ahead can provide a helpful clue if it goes over safely but he knows an unluckily-placed jam-up only has to happen to him once . . . Equally he will hold back speed before a dip until he can see the *bottom* of it is clear, not just that there is no one the other side. He reduces speed dramatically through villages, regardless of what limit is posted. Yet, he may be one of the fastest drivers wherever the road is safe. The essential thing is that his speed fluctuates continuously – ever adapting to changing circumstances. It is the weak, ineffectual driver who ploughs on at a constant speed, unaware of or unwilling to heed potential hazards.

As well as the need to read the road, speed-management demands accounting for other traffic. The ebb and flow of a typical traffic stream will mean you must be constantly varying your accelerator pressure to maintain your safe following distance. But that's not all. You cannot assume traffic ahead is moving at a safe speed. It's your own judgment that counts. If the guy ahead runs into some obstruction, do you want to smash into his rear?

Suppose you are in a flow of town traffic and you see parked cars ahead on your side. No one is coming the other way and the stream ahead moves out to pass those cars giving them a nice wide berth. Just before your turn to pass them comes, you notice another car pulling out from a hidden turning on the right, opposite the cars. Because of him, although there is still plenty of room, you are going to be forced to drive much closer to those parked cars, with the attendant dangers of carelessly opened doors, children running out between them, etc. Regardless of what drivers ahead may do, you must slow down quite drastically to retain stop-ability should trouble happen. Once the approaching car has passed, if the road is then clear, you can move out again slightly to give the remaining cars a wider berth, and speed up if you want to.

At higher speeds (and especially on motorways) stopping distances are less easy to visualise, and suggested following distances equally so. The 'Two Second' rule in the Highway Code can help. Whatever your speed, note the exact moment when the vehicle in front passes a prominent feature at the side of the road. Unless you pass that point AT LEAST two seconds (or a slow count of two) later – you are driving too close for your speed.

In the wet, make it a count of six. That will feel dramatic compared with what you see other drivers doing. Don't be fooled by ignorance. The principle which the Courts uphold should you run into the back of someone because they stop and you can't, is that it is your fault. No excuses are allowed.

Keeping your distance is no panacea on its own. All the

distance in the world is wasted if you are not quick enough to use it. Imagine yourself bowling along at 70 mph on a dual carriageway – or a motorway after passing your Test. It is no good staring at the brakelights of the car in front or of the one in front of that, at the expense of the *long view*.

Vital as the short view is, you must also look at what is happening in the traffic flow a good half-mile ahead.

If it is flowing smoothly, fine. But the instant you notice it getting knotted up, get ready to slow down or stop. Seize opportunities at curves, rises, or dips to capture this critical *long view*. When you lose it for a while as is bound to happen, increase your following distance accordingly, until you can see again. Remember the long view can save your life only if you see it.

HAND BOOK BACK TO YOUR INSTRUCTOR

BRIEFING

After looking over your Progress Chart, outline the lesson:-

1. Before you reach any busy streets in the town, you will call for a couple of Quick-Reaction Stops under modest braking, exactly as practised originally in Lesson 3. You will then take over and demonstrate several full Emergency Stops from progressively higher speeds. You will make them from as high as 40 mph which is higher than normally expected on the Test. The idea will be for him to see how the principles he has learnt translate into practice; and to be able to ask questions.

2. He will then drive again and you will call for some full Emergency Stops at random. Confirm that from now on the signal you have been using for a Quick-Reaction Stop is to mean a full Emergency Stop, and that as always, you will have checked all around before giving the signal. When he's done enough for the lesson, you will let him know so he can relax from his constant state of readiness. If it starts to rain, although you will still demonstrate, you will postpone *his* first full Emergency Stops for the safer dry roads of another day. Once he's experienced dry road stops, you will be taking in wet ones anyway – as soon as the weather obliges!

LESSON PLAN

STAGE 1 – Head for town via a quiet area where you can call for a Quick-Reaction Stop. Try it again if you are not fully satisfied with the first one.

STAGE 2 – Change over and demonstrate full Emergency Stops from 20 mph, 30 mph, and then 40 mph if conditions allow. Emphasise the huge difference in car control between the 20 mph stop and the 40 mph stop.

STAGE 3 – With your learner back at the wheel, keep him on quiet roads and ask him to stick to about 20 mph. At opportune moments, call for two or three Emergency Stops from this speed. If they are good, try a couple from no more than 30 mph. Then be sure to release him from his state of emergency preparedness! You will need to continue to practise in future lessons in order to reach and then maintain a high standard including, a little later, safe Emergency Stops on wet roads. In this first session, always give your signal when he is nicely settled on a straight road. In later repeats, give it whilst he is changing gear, or just after he has taken a corner, etc., etc. That's when emergencies occur!

STAGE 4 – Direct your learner further into the town traffic. Include traffic situations he has not met before, and watch him carefully. There shouldn't be any level of difficulty he can't tackle now. But do not prompt him unless he asks, or seems to be faltering. This is a tiring lesson the first time, so try to ensure your route enables you to arrive back home within the hour.

FURTHER PRACTICE

At the start of each repeat session, go through your Progress Chart and whittle down outstanding weaknesses so that you can select suitable routes for extra practice on them.

Repeat this lesson until you are confident that your learner is at or above Test standard. Blend in plenty of the Test manoeuvres from Lessons 5, 6 and 9. Keep practising the Emergency Stops until he is reacting fast and stopping confidently without undue skidding on both wet and dry surfaces. As confidence and ability grow, introduce rush-hour traffic too.

ASSESSMENT

Replay in discussion all that this lesson has added. Comment on strengths and weaknesses in anticipation, planning, maintaining the right following distance, and keeping tabs on the *long view*. Ask questions framed to elicit answers which prove concepts have sunk in.

NIGHT DRIVING

Unless you have been forced to start night driving already, you can begin it during a repeat of this lesson. Make your trainee check beforehand that all lights and indicators work and that all windows are spotless inside and out. Test him to see that he can work all vital controls and switches – such as wipers, de-mister, etc. – in the dark.

Instruct him to use main beam at all times when conditions allow, not just occasionally if he feels like it. This applies particularly on country roads to highlight pedestrians, bicycles, etc., far ahead, as well as to help people who may wish to overtake. (Overtakers run high risks trying to pass people who never use main beam; they shouldn't pass when they can't see far enough ahead, but they do.) Help him decide correctly just how early to dip, to avoid dazzling an oncoming driver and how soon to dip if catching someone up behind. If he is dazzling someone, tell him at once; it's too dangerous to wait until your learner realises.

Because he is new to it, your learner will probably drive a little slower at first than darkness makes necessary. For example, he may well become confused between all the lights in a busy town centre. Don't be afraid to give warnings where you might not by day. With his untrained night-eyes, he may easily miss noticing hazards such as pedestrians or cyclists. Alert him early but without sounding alarmed.

Judgment of distance and width is much more difficult at night. Again, you may have to prompt decisively in circumstances he would handle easily by day. Once he goes faster, you will undoubtedly have to remind him to restrict speed so that he can always stop within his headlamps-lit area, i.e. the distance he can see. You must watch that he focuses his eyes on his own side of the road and avoids getting dazzled by looking directly at the lights of approaching vehicles. Without losing touch with what is behind, he must also learn to prevent his eyes dwelling on his mirrors and being dazzled there. Remind him how to use the anti-dazzle interior mirror feature but warn him how much it distorts distance.

Normal eye-scanning is not enough when you arrive at a pitch-black junction or roundabout. There may be someone there even if there are no lights. As well as looking where his lights illuminate, teach your learner to let his eyes sweep the blackness beyond the edge of that area *slowly* but *surely*, so as to spot cyclists, joggers, or any poorly-lit vehicle. Even in twilight, your scanning power is reduced. Extra time must be taken. When you're out in the country at night, teach him to switch beams up and down at crossroads, hill-brows, etc., if no one is in sight. To let people know you are coming, it is a useful substitute for the horn.

PART THREE

THE TEST

Depending how quickly Test appointments come through in your area, you may feel your pupil should apply soon. Application forms are obtainable from main post offices. In the intervening time before your pupil's Test, you have lots more to do:-
* Additional reading for him.
* As much driving practice as you can both get time for.
* Mock Tests.
* Tips for Test day.

HAND BOOK BACK TO LEARNER

1

ADDITIONAL READING

FASTER DRIVING
This part investigates overtaking, driving out in the country, motorways and skidding. From it, I hope you will appreciate the dangers of trying to go too fast too soon, and, at any time in your driving life, of going faster than you personally can handle.

OVERTAKING ON THE OPEN ROAD
We here look at two-way single carriageway roads on which overtaking involves making use of the 'wrong' side whilst it is free of approaching traffic.

Three rules in the Highway Code jointly command that you allow others to pass if they want to. That means that if they need room to pull in front of you, you slow down to let them do so. Can you identify those three rules? Two are under 'Driving Along'. The third is under 'Overtaking'. Vow to yourself to abide by them before I warn you that when *you* are overtaking, you are going to come across drivers who wilfully disobey them. If you misjudge slightly and need to cut in at little 'cost' to them, these "monsters" will even speed up and cause you danger.

Your good example and consideration for others can play a big part in redressing danger on our roads caused by such mindless behaviour.

To overtake, your first prerequisite is to know there will be a gap to move back into, ahead of what you are passing. Without it, you must not begin. As we have just seen, you cannot assume that other drivers will create one for you.

That gap is one of several prerequisites which must all occur simultaneously at the moment you commit yourself to overtake. As you will be aware having been a passenger, there can be times where you have to stick behind another vehicle for miles before that occurs.

The other essential prior factors to consider are:-

1. Do you have sufficient extra acceleration available to pass quickly, bearing in mind whether or not the road may start to go uphill before you are back on your own side?
2. Is the clear stretch ahead on the opposite side of the road which you intend to use, long enough, even if a car hurtles over the horizon towards you at 100 mph? No one, not even a driver exceeding the speed limit, should ever have to slow down, still less, swerve because of your overtake.
3. Is anyone behind trying to overtake YOU? If there is, and he pulls out first, you cannot cut outwards in front of him.

The key to safe overtaking lies in being PREPARED to go, in keeping a running picture of how the factors above are falling into place. Then when the right moment opens up, you can go instantly.

As that moment looms near, for example with one last car to pass the other way, you slip into the right gear to maximise acceleration, and begin closing up on the vehicle in front. You begin your signal and pace your moving up so you will be 100% ready for pulling out to coincide with the clear stretch coming free. However, you time it so as not to get so close that you would then have to pull out at an acute angle.

Notice that you are not yet committed.

You may find repeatedly that as you reach this stage another oncoming car appears, or one of your prerequisite factors is now unfavourable, or that some unresolved doubt must be "listened to". But if you never PREPARE to overtake, most safe chances will slip through your fingers. However often you may be thwarted, you must then cancel your indicator and drop back. Always drop well back as explained below.

A good view ahead is essential to confirm that there will be a gap for you to slip back into on your own side and to confirm there will be a sufficiently long clear stretch on the opposite side for the pass. To gain that view, although you need to be closer than a normal following distance, you must hold well back from the car ahead. Available vision reduces dramatically once you get too close. You will with experience learn to judge the best distance back to be able to see clearly and yet be close enough to PREPARE quickly up to the ready-to-pull-out stage. That distance will depend upon speed, size of the vehicle ahead, terrain, etc. If you position yourself nicely through a bend, you can often grab the view you need where less imaginative drivers would be frustrated.

From your Highway Code under 'Overtaking' you need to commit to memory the list of places given where you MUST NOT overtake. Notice any one of them during your PREPARE stage and you must drop back and wait. Never let your self-discipline be found lacking on this.

Once committed to an overtake, do it rapidly as advocated by the Code. Minimise your time occupying the wrong side of the road. If you dawdle, you extend your exposure to oncoming traffic and errors of judgment. The delay increases the chance of reaching a MUST NOT overtake place before you can move in; the gap you are aiming to move into can shrink if your traffic stream slows down, and so on. *Things no one can foresee also happen.*

Overtake with a berth of at least a car door's width outside whatever you are passing, more if speeds are very high. Once past, move in without a split-second's unnecessary delay. All you must make sure is you don't force the driver you have overtaken to slow down. Do not wait to spy him in your mirrors as some so-called 'experts' do. Make a rapid glance over your left shoulder to confirm how soon you *can* pull across. By the time you do so, your mirrors will also be proving you are clear, but you will have gained several sweet seconds of safety.

How soon you can pull in will depend upon how quickly you have been overhauling the other vehicle. With experience, you build up a 'feel' for the relationship between speeds and timing. It is this experience learned in the right way that can save the day when – as inevitably sometimes happens – you have to cut in quickly in emergency. That day will come despite your best efforts. You will know then exactly how finely to judge it. Cutting in sharply is wrong but in an emergency it may be safer than a head-on smash.

Keep your right signal going during an overtake. Cancel it as you move in. Apart from on a motorway when it is useful, a left signal as you move in is normally superfluous. However, in a tight spot when you have to move in quickly, a signal can help remove doubt for all concerned.

If you think the person you are about to pass has no idea of it, give a toot on the horn or a headlight flash just before committing yourself. This should inform them but never assume it will!

A book cannot teach you how to judge relative speeds. Your instructor has to guide you to begin with. As well as the skills in timing already mentioned, he can prompt you on overtakes where, although there is traffic coming the other way, it is still so far off that you have time to get on with your pass. In this regard your own instructor may prefer to enlist the help of another friend more able to show you these special overtaking skills. This is no reflection upon your instructor's driving or teaching ability. It is simply a reflection on the reality that faster driving and overtaking is not everyone's desire. Plenty of safe drivers rarely overtake. But you will learn better here from someone long-experienced in maintaining safe high average speeds cross-country, someone to whom overtaking is a normal rather than exceptional experience.

For overtaking on those notorious three-lane roads seen in Lesson 7, the Highway Code says ". . . you have no more right to use the middle lane than a driver coming from the opposite direction". Equally, he has no more priority than you. Common sense prevails. If an oncoming driver is already using the middle lane, you wait. To pull out in the face of oncoming traffic would be pure recklessness. But if you are in the lane yourself, *never assume* the same kindness and sense in return. Be on guard for the maniac who feels entitled to try and force you over, perhaps into an earlier gap than the one you are heading for. Never play follow-my-leader, hoping a front overtaker will clear the way for you. Your exposure if he 'dives' into a gap or has a smash, is horrific. Driving in the middle lane, safety dictates always keeping closer to the stream you are passing than to the traffic going the other way.

DRIVING ON COUNTRY ROADS

Most driving instruction concentrates on town driving. However, my aim is to make you a safe all-rounder.

Disciplined speed-management must rule across country no less than in town. Tempted as you may be to whizz round a blind country bend, what happens if you find a pedestrian walking along your side just around the corner? (Assume there are no pavements and the road is narrow.) If it's too late to stop, then to pull out and steer round is the only option! But imagine there is a car coming the other way . . . !

Sooner or later most drivers find themselves in a pickle of this severity, though not always of their own making. So what can you learn from that story apart from the need to treat bends with respect? You can learn that if you are the driver coming the other way, then directly you see such a pedestrian, and even though he is walking on the other side of the road, you must slow down much more than just for the corner. You must be prepared for some clown to come zapping round the bend too fast and being forced to swing out into you to avoid the pedestrian. Pedestrians are too precious to leave to chance. Add a soft toot to alert the walker to the potential danger.

The Highway Code suggests you treat horses and other animals with respect and 'go slowly' when passing them in either direction. Even stop and let them pass you, if necessary. To attain the appropriate level of care, presume every horse you meet is a nervous thoroughbred at least until "stable" behaviour confirms you can relax a little.

In heavy rain, narrow country roads are much more prone to flooding than well-drained city roads. Expect flooding in dips but look out everywhere, especially at night when it's harder to see the water. If you hit a huge puddle on *one* side at speed, it can hurl your steering off up the bank. Where a big flood takes over the road, beware of the effect on your brakes. Once you have eased gently through the flooding, drive slowly for a few moments with your left foot lightly on the brake pedal. This will dry out the brakes. Otherwise the water can linger and give you a nasty brakeless shock when they are next needed.

MOTORWAYS

Although you are barred from motorway driving until after your Test, you MUST study it in your Highway Code, including the relevant section of the 'Law's Demands' at the back. The only way the examiner can discover what you know about using motorways is to ask you questions. So he will. Although you need to study it before your Test, what follows is written on the basis that you have recently passed.

First time out, pick a dry day at a quiet time. Get the 'feel' of motorway driving before venturing out of the left hand lane. Believe me, it is not just faster normal driving. Motorways have two, three, four, or sometimes more, lanes in each direction. You drive in the left hand lane. All the right hand lanes are for overtaking. Four lanes and more are unusual except where two motorways merge. Direction signs always give ample warning of which lane you need, and allow time for you to get into it. Take care the left lane you may be in doesn't split away for another destination. Sometimes keeping to the lefthandmost lane for the route you *do* want will mean temporarily being in a lane having additional ones to its left, whilst the motorway passes through a complex intersection with another one.

You MUST NEVER overtake on the left, except in a queue if the left hand lane happens to move before the right hand one. The hard shoulder always provided on the left is for emergency use (such as breakdowns) *only*. It is NOT a lay-by. However, it is sometimes brought into use to ease the congestion of nearby roadworks.

So that motorway traffic can flow uninterrupted, getting onto, or off, a motorway, is different. Direct crossings, junctions and right turns are eliminated. Traffic enters and leaves by means of "slip roads" which are always to the left. Thus you reach a destination to your right by driving off a slip road to your LEFT.

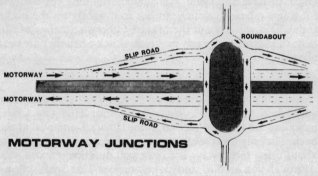

MOTORWAY JUNCTIONS

Fig. 32

The motorway slip road access is normally via a large roundabout above or below as in fig. 32. If you should miss your exit junction you must continue to the next junction before you can leave the motorway and return to your planned route. (Attempting to reverse or turn on the motorway is illegal and extremely dangerous.) However, if the next junction is with another motorway there will probably be no roundabout; there may only be a clover-leafed four-way convergence. You then have to carry on along one or other motorway to the next ordinary intersection before you can retrace your steps.

Since you are not allowed to stop for map reading, if you are driving alone it is essential to plan your exit point *before you join* the motorway. All exits are sequentially numbered to help.

As you enter the slip road to join a motorway you need to be in 2nd or 3rd gear while you look for a gap in left-hand-lane traffic. Depending on relative speeds when you spot a gap, you can thus be geared to accelerate as rapidly as necessary to merge smoothly into it. However, although sometimes you push ahead to slot in in front of another vehicle, just as often you will find it safer to hold your speed in check so as to slip in behind. If you see no gap, be prepared to stop just before the end of the slip road. You must then wait for a much longer gap in order to reach a normal left lane speed before the next vehicle coming along finds you are making him slow down.

Never lose sight of two questions:
1.   Will anyone ahead on the slip road have to stop?
2.   Is the traffic in the left hand lane of the motorway about to stop?

Both these things happen often. The inexperienced driver who forgets to LOOK IN FRONT as well as over his right shoulder can be fooled.

Because people drive faster, tricky situations arise faster on motorways. You must respond faster. You must counteract the fact that thinking-time in emergency is correspondingly reduced, by better long-range planning and higher concentration on what is happening in the *long view* ahead. You must use your mirrors constantly. Before you change lanes inwards or outwards, refer several times to your mirrors – including after you have started signalling. Vehicles hide in mirror blind-spots for miles; others roar up behind, catching you up at illegal speed. It takes more than a single casual look to assess how quickly someone coming up fast may be overhauling you. A rapid physical glance over your shoulder before you make your move should just confirm the facts.

That glance over the appropriate shoulder is also the only way you are going to spot another very common danger, the motorist heading for the same lane from the opposite side. He may be overhauling you fast and pulling from the outer right hand lane back to the middle one just as you intend to move out there. Or he may be joining off a slip road just as you are easing across from the middle, back to the left hand lane. In these situations, priority should go to the driver moving in from the right but that is of little consolation to him if the fellow trying to move out never sees him! In practice, both drivers need to be aware this can happen, and need that swift glance to be sure their manoeuvre is safe. It is for these sorts of reasons that I earlier suggested you should signal left after overtaking on a motorway. It can help prevent such troubles.

Lastly, when you come to drive on motorways you will hardly fail to notice how, as we saw on page 110, a common misunderstanding – here of the motorway rules – about using a middle lane, is wreaking havoc on these otherwise very safe roads. I hope you will always encourage better driving by good example.

SKIDDING

You will have probably seen just how lethal wet surfaces can be during Emergency Stop practice on the wet. (If you haven't yet had the chance to try one yourself from *slow* speed, be sure to have your instructor let you the next time it rains.)

On wet roads always increase your following distances to allow three to four times normal stopping margins. Reduce speeds generally by at least a third.

Excessive speed on wet roads, especially before storm water dissipates, leads to aquaplaning. The front wheels ski; they rise on the water, stop revolving and lose any vestige of steering. Only luck keeps the car on the road. Serious effects don't normally happen below 50 mph although they can certainly be noticeable.

Braking from any speed on loose surfaces, such as wet leaves, gravel, mud, etc. is doubly dangerous. You need to be aware that the loose materials stick to your tyres, intervening between them and the road; together they slide along the road surface because no tyre grip can reach it.

In winter there are the extra hazards of ice, black (hidden transparent) ice, and freezing rain. When they are about, to rely on any rule-of-thumb increase in safety margin is impracticable. Yes, still longer margins make sense, but you must do more if you are going to spot the first ice when it is forming. That's the time when people have major unexpected skids. Later, when everyone has realised the problem, is usually safer but see below. If you are driving in freezing weather and the temperature is dropping fast, make gentle brake tests from time to time when there is no one behind or coming. Instant wheel lock forbodes trouble. Take the hint if other people are crawling slowly, especially two-wheelers. Be warned if you have a minor skid of any kind. Once you know there is ice on a road, even if it only seems patchy, 10–15 mph can be maximum especially on stretches exposed to wind chill.

At every prospective stop – e.g. for a junction – begin exceedingly cautious braking, ten times earlier than normal. Then if you do skid, you at least have a margin in which hopefully to recover. It's worth noting that freezing rain can be so slippery that any steep downhill will be unsafe to attempt. Once snow is compacted and iced over, the same can apply.

Snow, and ice (and loose surfaces) all demand very, *very* gentle, almost imperceptible braking to start with. Even if speed is well below a jog, there can be times when there is little chance of stopping. The Emergency Stop braking and steering techniques from page 158 must be used immediately the car slides. Sometimes that's from the moment you touch the brake.

Your wheels will almost always finish a stop on ice or snow, locked for the last few feet (unless you release the brake). On fresh snow, the stop is helped a little because snowflakes build up and start having to be pushed along in front of the wheels. Making use of this factor by holding your brake on in the final stages of stopping, can therefore be something to try as a last resort. Moving on to fresh snow near the edge of the road may need to be part of that strategy. Provided it's not so deep you bog down in it, fresh snow will always provide greater traction and safety in any case. (With anti-lock brakes you should note that the snow-push effect above will not be so strong, if it's there at all.)

You can also skid through accelerating too fast. The driven wheels spin instead of moving the car. On a wet or greasy surface this can happen if you accelerate too fast away from stop, or if you over-accelerate round a bend, or if you bring in full power too sharply after changing into a lower gear.

On snow or ice, these effects are many times magnified. To be stuck, wheels spinning, unable even to start is a familiar sight. Or when you can move off, you often get bogged down as soon as you try to speed up or climb a hill.

If you have front wheel drive a manageable loss of steering control often attends this sort of skid. With rear wheel drive, unfortunately the back end of the car can attempt to snake round viciously. However, that would have to be quite an extreme skid. To scotch a wheelspin skid, snap your foot off the accelerator until it subsides; directly that happens you need to restore milder acceleration to help "balance" the car on its way. At the same time you should be straightening the steering on front wheel drive, or steering into the skid if rear wheel drive rear-end breakaway has begun. All these antics may not save you if traffic is "tight" around you. Indeed you may have to steer through a hedge rather than hit someone.

Skids develop through the "simple" act of cornering too fast, especially on slippery roads. The car veers towards the sharpest part of the bend. Loss of adhesion usually comes first to the front wheels (although it can be to the rear ones), or to all at once as near as makes no difference. (For the front wheels to slide first is more manageable, strange as that may seem. The tendency springs from deliberately built-in under-steer.) What constitutes "too fast" depends on conditions. You could get into trouble at 20 mph on ice, yet take the same corner at 60 mph in the dry. A bend with a deep camber dipping down to the outside edge and thus working against you, will fool you at the same speed that a similar bend with the camber banked towards you can be taken safely.

You have already learned that braking must always be completed before a corner so that the bend can be taken under slight acceleration. In slippery conditions, as well as cutting overall speed, this technique becomes crucial and may need further refinement. Your slight re-acceleration must be nowhere near enough to provoke wheelspin.

Notice how hard-braking causes the car to nose-down, whereas fierce acceleration does the opposite. The worst thing you can do mid-bend at high speed is swap abruptly from nose-down to nose-up. Centrifugal force is already trying to hurl the car off the road. A sudden shift in the centre of gravity as well can easily trigger a skid.

All this should, I hope, lead you to appreciate that disciplined speed-management before bends is the essential safe cornering ingredient. Recovery from any skid can never be guaranteed but this type, caused by excessive cornering speed is perhaps the most unpredictable. To recover, you must instantly release the brakes at least temporarily to unlock the wheels (or come off the accelerator for a moment if you are still going full tilt). Get your steering straight, or steer "into the skid" if appropriate, at the same time. All the while, you have to be thinking quickly whether you should opt to leave the road anyway (if you haven't already!), or whether you can save yourself without danger to others. If it's the latter, hopefully your initial actions will have preserved the chance to try. Correct what remains of the skid in the ways described earlier, depending whether steering clear of danger is now the dominant factor, or you are still desperately trying to stop, or you need to curb wheelspin.

Apart from understanding your lack of stopping power, driving on snow demands special techniques just in order to keep going.

1. Always start off in the highest gear you can, for example, 3rd on the flat; this is your best way to prevent wheelspin digging you in.
2. In queues, use timing to avoid coming to a standstill except where it is unavoidable.
3. Whenever possible choose where you do have to stop carefully, so you don't have to re-start on an uphill, etc.
4. Change down, before going up a hill, to the highest gear which will still take you to the top (a change halfway up can trigger wheelspin).
5. For best traction it can be worth trying fresh snow away from rutting (but avoid kerbs, etc.).
6. The 10–15 mph maximum speed suggested for ice earlier will be plenty for most snow conditions; on fresh snow on a straight level empty road, 25–30 mph ought to be tops.

HAND BOOK BACK TO INSTRUCTOR

2

FASTER DRIVING IN PRACTICE

When your learner has read to here, take him out with yourself at the wheel and show him some overtaking, some brisk open road country driving and some fast motorway driving. During the drive and later at home you can discuss and explain what he has learned about skidding. You should show him an Emergency Stop from high speed, i.e. 65 mph plus; it is vital for him to witness the hugely increased distances that it takes to stop from speed. Figures on paper don't give a proper impression at all. As explained on page 173, you may decide the above demonstration can be better handled by someone who normally drives faster than you do yourself.

Do not suggest that your learner should suddenly jump in the driving seat afterwards and put his foot down! Your repeats of the earlier lessons should carry on now from where they left off.

3

MOCK TESTS

It is worth giving your learner the experience of three or four mock Tests. Each time, choose a route which will take about 40 minutes and include: traffic lights, roundabouts, one-way systems, steep hills, turns and junctions (including some on hills if possible), pelican and zebra pedestrian crossings. Plan ahead where you will ask him to move off from behind a parked vehicle, carry out an Emergency Stop, start on a hill, reverse into a limited opening, and conduct a three point turn.

Explain to your "candidate" that you will direct him along the route and ask when you want specific manoeuvres like the Emergency Stop, or three point turn, but you will say little otherwise. This will simulate the position of the examiner – who is not allowed to engage in casual conversation. At the end you will ask questions on the Highway Code.

Prepare a "Test" checklist like fig. 33 to have in front of you.

MOCK TEST CHECKLIST ✔ = at or above an acceptable standard ✗ = sub-standard	Date of mock test			
EYESIGHT				
PRECAUTIONS BEFORE STARTING ENGINE				
MOVING AWAY CORRECTLY				
USE OF GEARS				
USE OF MIRRORS				
USE OF CLUTCH				
USE OF FOOTBRAKE/HANDBRAKE				
USE OF ACCELERATOR				
STEERING				
POSITIONING IN THE ROAD				
GIVING ADEQUATE CLEARANCE TO PARKED VEHICLES				
SIGNALLING				
MAKE REASONABLE PROGRESS				
AVOID UNDUE HESITANCY				
STOPPING UNDER CONTROL IN EMERGENCY				
REGULATE SPEED WITH PROPER CARE				
OBSERVATION AT JUNCTIONS				
ACT ON SIGNAL GIVEN BY AUTHORISED PERSON				
GIVING WAY TO VEHICLES				
GIVING WAY TO PEDESTRIANS				
OBSERVING SPEED LIMITS				
OBSERVING TRAFFIC SIGNS				
STOPPING IN A SAFE POSITION				
STARTING ON A HILL				
REVERSING ROUND A CORNER				
THREE POINT TURN				
AWARENESS OF OTHER ROAD USERS				
SHOWING COURTESY AND CONSIDERATION				
HIGHWAY CODE QUESTIONS				

Fig. 33

HIGHWAY CODE QUESTIONS

To complete each mock Test you could use questions from this book, or make some up yourself. Alternatively you can find a mine of sample questions in companion Paperfront "Highway Code Questions and Answers" by John Humphries.

ASSESSMENT

The standards expected for all except two of the items on the mock Test checklist have already been explained. It should be no problem to mark for competence in them, and to discuss improvements needed. But how do you evaluate "make reasonable progress" and "avoid undue hesitancy"? If your learner can generally keep up with events during a forty-minute run in rush-hour, you need have no worries. But if he gets hooted at for dithering at junctions or never reaches the speed limit to keep up with urban traffic, forget the real Test for the time being. He probably needs five times the practice he's done so far. Fear of being able to control the car may be the problem just as much as lack of practice. Overhauling the car control manoeuvres may need to be the priority.

4

TIPS FOR TEST DAY

Make sure your candidate remembers the 'L' plates, his provisional licence, appointment card, and glasses or contact lenses if needed. Early in the day, give the car the standard weekly check-over of Lesson 4. I hope we can assume the road tax and insurance didn't expire yesterday!

Your candidate can drive there, although if it is more than an hour's drive, it may be best to share the task. Plan to arrive 10–15 minutes early to allow your candidate time to visit the lavatory for comfort and to smarten himself up before the examiner calls his name.

RETURN BOOK TO CANDIDATE

5

WHAT TO EXPECT

Your mock Tests will have included all that the real Test demands of you. So there should be no surprises.

People say driving examiners are biased. This is untrue. When I sat my driving Test a good many years ago, my instructor resigned himself to my failure. Unknown to me, my examiner had just returned to work after a serious crash on a Test. The repaired car was the very one in which I was sitting my Test! I passed. That says a lot for examiner objectivity and impartiality.

Some say examiners try to fail younger drivers. I was 22 years old when I took the Test, so I suppose I had the benefit of maturity. However, my daughter passed her Test, first attempt, just four months after her seventeenth birthday. You will probably hear many dubious opinions about driving examiners. Treat them as bunkum, designed to paper over someone else's inability to pass.

Once you have that precious Pass you'll no doubt be tempted to get into the car and roar off. Take heed! You are not transformed into an expert driver simply because you pass a forty-minute Test. The examiner's blessing does NOT carry with it all the wisdom accumulated over years of driving by the safest drivers. Your Test was your first experience of sole responsibility. A safe reputation has to be earned over a lifetime, learning and improving as you go. No one ever dare say they know it all!

All that remains is to wish you pleasure and safety on the road. I hope this book has been of value to you. If it has, please tell your friends. My publishers and their editorial team will be pleased to hear your suggestions for improvements to it, or to answer driving questions if you care to write in with them.

INDEX

OUR PUBLISHING POLICY

HOW WE CHOOSE

Our policy is to consider every deserving manuscript and we can give special editorial help where an author is an authority on his subject but an inexperienced writer. We are rigorously selective in the choice of books we publish. We set the highest standards of editorial quality and accuracy. This means that a *Paperfront* is easy to understand and delightful to read. Where illustrations are necessary to convey points of detail, these are drawn up by a subject specialist artist from our panel.

HOW WE KEEP PRICES LOW

We aim for the big seller. This enables us to order enormous print runs and achieve the lowest price for you. Unfortunately, this means that you will not find in the *Paperfront* list any titles on obscure subjects of minority interest only. These could not be printed in large enough quantities to be sold for the low price at which we offer this series. We sell almost all our *Paperfronts* at the same unit price. This saves a lot of fiddling about in our clerical departments and helps us to give you world-beating value. Under this system, the longer titles are offered at a price which we believe to be unmatched by any publisher in the world.

OUR DISTRIBUTION SYSTEM

Because of the competitive price, and the rapid turnover, *Paperfronts* are possibly the most profitable line a bookseller can handle. They are stocked by the best bookshops all over the world. It may be that your bookseller has run out of stock of a particular title. If so, he can order more from us at any time—we have a fine reputation for "same day" despatch, and we supply any order, however small (even a single copy), to any bookseller who has an account with us. We prefer you to buy from your bookseller, as this reminds him of the strong underlying public demand for *Paperfronts*. Members of the public who live in remote places, or who are housebound, or whose local bookseller is unco-operative, can order direct from us by post.

FREE

If you would like an up-to-date list of all *Paperfront* titles currently available, send a stamped self-addressed envelope to
ELLIOT RIGHT WAY BOOKS, BRIGHTON RD.,
LOWER KINGSWOOD, SURREY, U.K.